GLORY ROAD

GLORY ROAD

My Story of the 1966 NCAA Basketball
Championship and How One Team
Triumphed Against the Odds and
Changed America Forever

COACH DON HASKINS

WITH DAN WETZEL

HYPERION

NEW YORK

Library of Congress Cataloging-in-Publication Data

Haskins, Don.
Glory road : my story of the 1966 NCAA bas-
ketball championship and how one team triumphed
against the odds and changed America forever /
Don Haskins with Dan Wetzel.
p. cm.
ISBN 1-4013-0791-4 (alk. paper)
1. Haskins, Don, 1930– 2. Basketball coaches—
United States—Biography. 3. University of Texas at
El Paso—Basketball. I. Wetzel, Dan. II. Title.

GV884.H26A29 2006
796.323'092—dc22
[B]   2005050349

Hyperion books are available for special promotions
and premiums. For details contact Michael Rentas,
Assistant Director, Inventory Operations, Hyperion,
77 West 66th Street, 11th floor, New York,
New York 10023, or call 212-456-0133.

FIRST EDITION

5 7 9 10 8 6 4

For my wife, Mary
My four sons, Mark, Stephen, Brent, and David
And my three grandsons, Cameron, John-Paul,
and Dominick
—*Don Haskins*

For my wife, Jan, and daughter, Allie,
thanks for making my life
—*Dan Wetzel*

CONTENTS

FOREWORD

The night of March 19, 1966, will always be thought of whenever basketball is discussed as the defining moment in the career of Don Haskins. This of course was the night that his team starting five black players defeated all-white Kentucky, 72–65, for the National Championship. This was the first time a team with five black starters had accomplished the ultimate in college basketball and Don has received tremendous acclaim over the years for being a pioneer on behalf of the black athlete in basketball. This is deservedly so, but there is also tremendous irony in this approach to Don and his career. There is no one that I have ever known who was more racially color-blind than Don Haskins. He simply played the best players that he could recruit without giving any thought whatsoever to their color, and this to me far more defines the man than anything else about that particular game. The way those players and that team played the defensive end of the floor throughout the forty minutes of that game defined Don as a coach rather than the color of his players' skin.

At the beginning of that 1965–66 college basketball season I did not know very much about either Texas Western College or Don Haskins as a coach, and I am sure Don could say the exact same thing about me as a coach and the Army basketball team. During the course of that season, however, as Texas Western won game after game running off a string of twenty-three straight, I paid more and more attention to the team and its coach. The first thing I found out was that Don had played at Oklahoma A&M for Henry Iba. This immediately got my attention because Coach Iba was not only one of the most highly respected coaches ever to be involved with basketball, but perhaps the most demanding of all. A player who played for him had to possess a mental toughness far beyond that necessary to play for most coaches.

The first time I was around Don I saw two things immediately. There was no nonsense with this guy; none with him personally, nor would he put up with any around him. The second thing that struck me immediately was just how extremely intelligent the guy was.

Even though Kentucky featured a fast-paced offense, the

championship game was completely controlled by Texas Western's defense and the way they applied pressure to the ball and helped out against driving and postplay. I had never seen anybody play defense better than Don's team did that night. While that particular game brought Don Haskins and Texas Western to the attention of everyone in America interested in basketball, it was the next thirty-two seasons that truly defined Don Haskins as a coach.

El Paso was not created for Don Haskins, but Don Haskins was certainly made for El Paso. El Paso, founded in 1536, is one of the great western heritage cities in our history. It is a town early on full of tough people in a tough environment. Among its inhabitants have been oil field roughnecks, miners, cattlemen, cotton farmers, outlaws, and lawmen, all giving El Paso one of the richest and most colorful heritages of any of our western frontier or border towns. These independent, tough-minded, hardworking, and warmhearted people in El Paso immediately recognized the blond-haired young coach from Oklahoma as a kindred spirit. The relationship during the ensuing years between Miner fans and their coach, who they nicknamed the Bear, was as strong as any similar relationship ever in college athletics. My nickname for him has always been El Paso Ed. This comes from the 1972 Olympic Trials held at the Air Force Academy. It was Coach Iba's third time to be the head coach of the Olympic team, Don was an assistant coach, and I was there to help with the trials. One night we were sitting at a restaurant bar in downtown Colorado Springs and a guy came over and wanted somebody to shoot pool with him. He said, "Somebody told me you were all coaches. One of you must be able to shoot pool." Nobody said anything and finally Don said, "Aw, I'll get up and shoot a game or two with you." I think they played for a dollar and Don lost, and they played for two dollars and Don lost, and then they started playing for five dollars and in about forty minutes Don won one hundred and twenty-five dollars. He came back and sat down, looked at me, and said, "I can beat the guy left-handed." This was after the movie with Jackie Gleason and Paul Newman, *The Hustler*, came out with Gleason playing the legendary pool shark Minnesota Fats. I had a great nickname to hang on Don because of his pool prowess, which was El Paso Ed, and any time that I would call him I would always just leave a message that Ed called.

The thirty-two seasons that Don coached after winning the National Championship in 1966 were the definition of him as a coach. El Paso, while it has a tremendous American heritage as well as wonderful people, is a very difficult place to recruit to. It is not a city that has a lot of homegrown basketball talent, nor does that region of the state of Texas. If you check closely, you will find that those schools that have done well year after year in college football or basketball are located in populated areas where kids are going to grow up wanting to come to that particular school. This was certainly not the case for players who played for Don at Texas Western and later at UTEP after the school's name changed. There is no doubt in my mind that Don did more with a particular situation than anybody who has ever coached college basketball.

His teams continued to be very tough to play against. They won league championships and league tournaments and participated in a lot of postseason play in both the NCAA tournament and NIT. I don't think college basketball has ever seen another coach who could have had the continual success in El Paso that Don had. His way of coaching was an almost fanatical adherence to the principles of defensive play that he learned at Oklahoma A&M under Henry Iba. The theme of his offense was to handle the ball without making mistakes and get good shots. He never wavered in his devotion to these principles and that enabled him, along with his unbending determination to get the most out of his players, to establish a consistently outstanding basketball program in a locality where it just shouldn't have been able to happen.

The only interruption to Don's career in El Paso came when he entered into a state of temporary insanity and took the coaching job at the University of Detroit for a day or two in 1971. When I heard that he was taking the Detroit job, all I could picture was Don in downtown Detroit calling coyotes, shooting doves, and driving around in his pickup with four shotguns and Lo, his Chinese hunting buddy.

Henry Iba, one of the truly legendary coaches of any sport in America's athletic history, turned out more coaches than anyone who has ever been involved with the game. While many of those coaches enjoyed great success, none remains closer to the principles taught by Mr. Iba or to the man himself than Don Haskins. Don once paid me a great compliment by telling me that I needed to know that the "old man," meaning Mr. Iba, really liked me. He said this as though he was kind of surprised that Mr. Iba would feel that way and I looked at Don and said, "Well, he likes you, doesn't he?"

Henry Iba was the toughest and most dignified of men. He was a brilliant pioneer in the game of basketball and everyone who has followed him has, knowingly or not, utilized the principles that he taught and developed regarding defensive play. I doubt if the word "dignified" will ever be used to describe Don or myself. I think perhaps that's why we had a particular appeal to Mr. Iba, because of things we might have done or said that he would have never thought of either doing or saying but deep down enjoyed. I always felt that he thought Don and I needed a little special guidance from him.

I mentioned the great part that the city of El Paso played in the history and development of the western part of the United States. There is no doubt in my mind, however, that the gruff, fiercely independent, and loyal coach who directed the Miner teams for thirty-eight seasons will go down as not only the most memorable of all the great personalities that have passed through El Paso over all the years, but the single individual who has contributed the most to the recognition of that city and that university throughout the country and the world. I have always admired him as a coach, not only for the way he taught the game, but for the tremendous love that he has for basketball. Every player that played for Don was able to take things with him throughout the rest of his life that would enable him to have an advantage over anybody that he was competing against in any walk of life. I have tremendous respect for Don as a man because of his honesty, intelligence, and his unwavering loyalty to people that have been a part of his life, exhibited nowhere more significantly than his relationship with Coach Iba. There is no one I have ever met that I take greater pride in calling a friend than Don Haskins. The final epitaph to his career should be Frank Sinatra singing "I Did It My Way," and no one ever did it better than Don Haskins did.

Bob Knight
June 27, 2005
Lubbock, Texas

GLORY ROAD

LEGEND

The wind chill was thirty degrees below zero in Ames, Iowa. One of those brutal, frozen, brittle days in the snow-packed upper Midwest in 1996. The radio kept saying to make sure you kept a candle and a blanket in your car, that way you could survive a couple days if you drove off the road and into a snow bank.

Presumably, by then, someone might find you.

There is cold and there is cold. Which is why when Tim Floyd, the Iowa State coach at the time whom I was in town interviewing for a magazine article, pulled his warm car into the parking lot of the Hilton Coliseum and eyeballed the frigid three-hundred-foot walk to the door, he just shook his head.

Floyd was from Mississippi and had spent a long portion of his career in El Paso, Texas. So he pulled the car back on the road and we drove around Ames, just to stay warm, just to avoid the weather for a few hours until it was time for practice. He began regaling me with stories about his colorful old boss at the University of Texas at El Paso, Don Haskins. We wound up driving around—Tim talking, me listening—for nearly two hours.

I can look back and say I've never been more thankful to have been stuck in the middle of an arctic blast.

"We go on a recruiting trip to little Zwolle, Louisiana," Floyd said that day. "We are flying out of Shreveport the next morning and are staying in some little hotel. Coach wasn't much for fancy hotels; he liked motel-type places, where you can park in front of your door. Simple. Next to the hotel is a little old run-down bar with a neon cowboy boot kicking.

"Coach sees it though and gets excited. This is his kind of place. 'Let's go in for a beer, Tim,' he says. Damn, I'm thinking, we have an early flight, but what are you going to do? It's pretty empty in there, a couple guys in back playing pool, five dollars a game. We sit down and are talking recruiting when Coach goes over and puts a quarter down on the pool table.

"One of the guys gets a little short with Coach and says, 'Hey, buddy, we're playing for money here, you still wanna play?' Coach is taken aback by the tone, so he says all innocently, 'Oh, I guess that'll be OK.' Coach's turn comes up and the guy says, 'We want to play for ten dollars a game now.' Coach is bothered now, but he just says, 'Oh, I guess that'll be OK.' Coach was in his late fifties at this point, he slowly gets over to the table and they begin playing.

"He beats the first guy by one ball," said Floyd, now coach at the University of Southern California. "Then the next guy gets up and Coach beats him by one ball. And on and on. Back and forth these guys keep trying and Coach keeps beating them by just one ball and then raising the bet— he calls it 'sprinkling corn in the field.' He winds up winning about twenty games in a row.

"Finally, Coach decides it's time to leave. Now, you could tell these two didn't have much; this is a poor bar in a poor town. They bit off more than they could chew. They look depressed. Coach had wiped them out of a week's pay or something. So Coach has all their money, a few hundred dollars, in his hand and he walks back over to the pool table, throws it down, and says, 'You best be careful who you gamble with in the future.' Then without saying another word, he just walks out of the bar."

I'd spent eight years as a national college basketball writer for a variety of magazines and Web sites. During this time I'd gotten to know just about every coach in the country. It has become an increasingly glitzy business, where Armani suits have overtaken American substance, where coaches, without even realizing the absurdity of it, began referring to themselves as "CEOs," where some spoke glowingly that "perception equals reality." This was a business where image had, indeed, become everything and ego was everywhere.

Except, apparently, out in west Texas, where Haskins was quietly winding down his Hall of Fame career. I knew the name and knew the story of 1966, but I didn't know much else. His teams by then were good, fundamentally sound, overachieving clubs, but with over three hundred Division I programs to cover, UTEP just wasn't as high of a priority as Kentucky, Duke, or Arizona. Like most in the national media, I was finding it easy to overlook UTEP.

But here was the John Wayne of basketball, a hustler, a hard guy, a legend who didn't want anyone, anywhere to know it. How tough was the man they called the Bear? In 1996 he started to have chest pains during halftime of a game, and when the paramedics came he refused to be wheeled out of the arena. Instead, he got up and walked to the ambulance. The next day he had quintuple bypass surgery.

He was in El Paso because the people and the media left him alone. He could have gone to bigger schools, where he would have had the resources to reach the Final Four every year, but he was content where he was, coaching and teaching without the fanfare. In a cutthroat business, this contentment was rare.

He was comfortable in El Paso because El Paso was comfortable with him. He wore a clip-on tie for games. His truck had guns in it and, occasionally, coyote carcasses in the bed ("They're payin' seventy-five dollars for a skin," he'd explain). Hustle a game of pool at some big, self-important university and you might get fired. But do it at UTEP and you are beloved. Even after the school named its 12,000-seat arena after him—the Don Haskins Center—he refuses to call it by anything but its original name, the Special Events Center.

I suspected that the coaches who kept justifying their $1.1 million salaries by explaining to me that their basketball program was "the front porch of the university" probably wouldn't be so humble. This was a guy I didn't just want to meet, but someone I needed to meet.

"You've got to go down there," said Floyd. "But you better find a way to get into his truck. That's where the stories are told. You aren't getting much of an interview if you can't get into the truck."

So I went; first as a journalist and later, after Haskins retired in 1999, I returned as a friend. And I got into that GMC truck, which I usually shared with a couple bottles of whiskey on the floor. I wound up going back there over and over to the point where my official favorite vacation destination in America was the unlikely location of old El Paso.

Needless to say, we made for an unusual friendship. He grew up in Oklahoma, I'm from Boston. We are separated in age by forty-two years. He enjoys mimicking (or butchering) my accent. I laugh when he calls a heavy rain "a frog strangler." He almost keeled over when he heard I had never shot a rifle in my life—this was after he, at the age of seventy-one, had just coolly killed a rattlesnake we had happened upon while walking around the desert. Of course, I think he was proud when on my first shot I absolutely blew the hell out of an empty Budweiser can.

"Yeah, you're a damn natural," he said.

What I found in El Paso was not just a friend but an American original, a man of principle and profundity, someone you could learn from by just sitting around with him at a little dive at two in the afternoon. On one of my first trips to El Paso we walked in through the back door of a rickety bar, the kind of place you can drive by a hundred times without even noticing, let alone think of patronizing. Ten or twelve Mexican day workers lined the wooden front bar, heads sort of sagging.

The most famous El Pasoan of all time called the lady behind the bar by her first name, bought a round of Buds for the house (total bill: twelve dollars, he left eight dollars as a tip), and then led me over to a small booth. Everyone in the place tipped their hat at Haskins, mumbled "Coach," and then stayed to themselves.

"See," he said, surveying the scene like it was heaven on earth, like he had just scored a prime table at Spago in Beverly Hills. "No one bothers you in this place."

We've never been to the elite spots in town, such as the grill room at the El Paso Country Club. Haskins referred to the Mesa Avenue restaurant Jaxon's—an Applebee's-like place—as "too fancy." Most of his friends, many of whom have become my friends, were simple blue-collar workers, often Mexican immigrants.

Unless you've been to El Paso, you can't fathom how big Don Haskins is, his presence looming larger than the Franklin Mountains that cut through the city. In west Texas Haskins is king in a region with few celebrities. He could have sipped the fine wine, could have dined on steak so succulent that you can cut it with a fork, could have had every rich oil baron in the area kissing his ass and inviting him to dinner parties.

Instead he likes drinking in dark, dank holes-in-the-wall. As much as he felt being enshrined in the Naismith Basketball Hall of Fame an honor, he's still a bit ornery that he had to wear a tuxedo to the ceremony. A good lunch is an oversized burrito in some local bakery that has no name and where no one speaks English. He knows what it's like to have significant action on a downhill eight-foot putt. A nice afternoon is a drive around the desert, stopping only to call coyotes. He can be approached by any old soul and he'll engage that person in conversation like he was the president of the United States.

He freely passes out extra money to honest people who have fallen a bit behind. He never tips less than thirty percent. He uses whatever connections he has with the wealthy to organize major relief efforts to poor villages on the other side of the Rio Grande, a humanitarian project he keeps a secret and never shares with the media. He can teach you the most simple of life's lessons in the most simple of ways.

It is one thing to be blue collar, to be salt of the earth. It is entirely another thing to choose to stay that way when fame and fortune and the so-called fabulous life present themselves to you. Don Haskins is the real McCoy, a once-in-a-lifetime slice of Americana.

Oh, and could he ever coach basketball.

"The people who understand what coaching is," Bob Knight told me one day, "the people who really know what great coaching is, are all going to talk about Don Haskins."

In thirty-seven years he never coached a single prep All-

American, the ultratalented recruits who consistently fuel the nation's best college programs. He had one junior college All American, but he graduated way back in 1964. He won 719 games and made twenty-one appearances in either the NCAA tournament or NIT without those kinds of players. His specialty was taking raw talents and teaching them how to play the game, routinely turning projects into players and players into pros. He was annually getting more out of less. I'm not saying John Wooden or Dean Smith couldn't have won 719 in El Paso, but Haskins certainly could have the record they did in Westwood or Chapel Hill.

But it was his decision to be the first college coach to start five black players that is his claim to fame. It was an historic, courageous decision that can't be minimized; no matter how often Haskins has tried. Not only did it change the course of basketball, but he did it (whether he admits it or not) with repercussions waiting. No small thing for a then thirty-five-year-old with a wife and four kids to feed.

"He risked his career by doing it," said Harry Flournoy, a cocaptain on that 1966 team. "If we hadn't won he might have gotten fired because a lot of people didn't think you could win with five black starters. If he were fired, then where would he have gone? Most colleges wouldn't have taken him."

Back then, there was a simple coaching axiom. You can play two blacks at home, three on the road, and four if you were losing. But never, ever five at once. That would get you fired. That would draw the wrong kind of attention. In the South, teams were all white. So when Haskins won the 1966

NCAA title by starting five blacks and playing seven altogether against all-white University of Kentucky, everything
changed. Pat Riley, a player on the opposing UK team, would
later call it "the Emancipation Proclamation of 1966." Others
referred to it as basketball's Brown v. Board of Education.

"The next year black kids throughout the South got calls
from schools saying they were now open," said Nolan
Richardson, one of Haskins's former players who, in 1994 as
coach of Arkansas, would become just the second African-
American coach ever to win an NCAA title. "He literally got
thousands and thousands of black kids scholarships."

And Haskins got death threats and hate mail.

"Most of them started the same way," he frowned. "Dear
Nigger Lover."

I've spent hundreds and hundreds of hours with the man,
and if you don't ask about 1966 then he doesn't mention it.
It's ancient history to him.

"I just played my best players," he's told anyone who
would listen for decades.

None of us want to believe him, but maybe we should
start trying.

Haskins doesn't want the glory. He agreed to be a part of
Disney's *Glory Road* movie only because Hollywood would
have made it without his permission anyway. He agreed to
write this book because he wants everyone to know the
truth—that he wasn't a racial pioneer or a civil rights hero, he
was just a simple coach seeking victory.

He is really, truly writing a book, honest to goodness, to

make sure he gets less credit. He doesn't want to be "some damn hero."

When we started working on this book together, he lectured me that he didn't want "any braggin' at all." This was after he found out I had written the following, supposedly boastful line: "I was a good free-throw shooter in high school."

"I don't want the word 'I' to appear in the book," he declared.

"It is an autobiography, how the hell do you expect the word 'I' not to appear?"

"Well, damn, it, I thought you were the genius writer."

That's Haskins though. Whether we were driving around in his truck, getting breakfast at the Sunset Inn in El Paso, a drink at the Sheepherder in Dell City, Texas, or talking on the phone, comparing college football picks, he is self-deprecating and hysterical. He is out of some other world. In retirement he cares about hunting, fishing, and family. And about little else.

He is completely out of touch with pop culture. He hasn't been to an actual theater since *Patton* in 1970. ("Some kids threw popcorn. Never went back.") He was once reading a front-page newspaper story about the death of a beloved and quite famous children's television star and demanded to know, "Who the hell is Mr. Rogers?"

This movie and this book are going to be interesting for Haskins. With any luck, America will discover the hero he is (no matter his protests) and celebrate him for it. The purpose of this book is to allow Haskins to tell his side of what happened in 1966 and also to allow people to get to know the personality that is as memorable as the accomplishments.

This country is searching for genuine characters, people who believe in something and stand up for it. Don Haskins is one of them. If anything can come out of that movie and this book, I hope that discovery is it. Just the way Tim Floyd told me to go find out about Haskins, I hope everyone else will.

What follows is his story in his words, just how you might hear it if we could ever get you into the truck for one of those long drives around the desert that always ends with a couple of cold beers in a middle-of-nowhere bar.

TWO

ENID, OKLAHOMA

The main thoroughfare that cuts through El Paso is Interstate 10.
From the east it rolls in from the desert, cuts past massive Fort Bliss,
wraps around the Franklin Mountains, through downtown, up near
UTEP, and eventually out through the suburban neighborhoods to
the west and into New Mexico, where more desert awaits. It is near
UTEP that I-10 offers a most poignant view toward the South—
Ciudad Juarez.

The Rio Grande is nothing but a slim, shallow river in these
parts, dividing America and the dream it represents from Mexico and
the dreams it has. From high on I-10, surrounded by the wealth of

the United States, the view of Juarez is stark and unforgettable. The homes are small, shoddy shacks, the roads made of dirt, clotheslines are strung through yards. This is to see abject poverty and a sense of political and economic hopelessness—a first world window into third world reality.

"I don't think," said Haskins softly as we drove past that view one day in his GMC truck, "that I've ever gotten used to that view."

Being born in America down here is the luck of the draw, winning the genetic lottery of winding up on one side of the river and not the other.

"You see that and you know Mexicans and Americans aren't any different," he said. "And you can understand why so many of them fight to get across the border. They are fighting to make it. To get a better life. How could you grow up in one of those little homes, look across at all of these big homes, all this money every day, and not try to cross the river?

"That's why I don't look down on anyone. Never have. It's why I relate to a lot of different people, of all races."

He paused.

"Besides, it ain't like I am from the upper crust myself . . ."

■

I was born in Enid, Oklahoma, in 1930. When it comes to times and places to get yourself born, this was probably not one of the best. The 1930s are best remembered for the Great

Depression. Oklahoma in the 1930s is best remembered for this incredible drought that turned the state into "the Dust Bowl." Things were so dry in some parts of the state that when the wind came sweeping down the plains, giant dirt clouds would form overhead. When it came to depressed places during a depressed time, Enid, Oklahoma, was a gold medal contender. It was so tough being an Okie back then that a lot of people decided not to be one anymore, and moved, just like John Steinbeck wrote in *The Grapes of Wrath,* focusing on all the dusty ole boys who hightailed it to California for a supposedly better life.

Not all of us left, though. Even though times were tough and money tight, it was possible to squeak out a living, but everyone had to work. Everyone in the family had to do whatever they could to help out—in our case, that meant not just my father Paul and mother Opal, but my younger brother Jerry and me. At the time, I had no idea about our unique place in history because when you are a kid, you know only what you know. I didn't know we had it that bad. In a lot of ways, I thought we had it great.

Enid is a small town in the northern part of the state. It was a nice, if unremarkable, place surrounded by wheat fields. It is right in the middle of the state's famed tornado alley and boy, was it flat. You could go bowling outside. It was the kind of place you could sit on your front porch and watch your dog run away . . . for three days. You could stand on top of a can of soup and see Colorado. And was there dust? More than you could believe.

During the Great Depression my family was lucky. My father was my hero and he had a steady job driving a truck for the Failing's Supply Company in Enid. A job like that was rare. He wasn't paid much, but we were thankful, I'll tell you that. The Depression was something else. I don't think most Americans today can even fathom the life we had. If the economy goes into a recession for one month now everyone starts hollerin'. But back then, people died from starvation. And it lasted for years. So when I say I was lucky because we never went hungry, I mean it. We weren't eating T-bones though. Most of what we got came from our garden. I remember a lot of beans and corn. I remember doing a lot of hoeing. My dad would hunt for food, not for sport, but we were primarily vegetarians—by necessity, not choice.

The best thing that happened during the Depression, of course, was President Roosevelt, who in my home was something close to a god. You wouldn't want to get in an argument with my dad about President Roosevelt or there would be a fistfight. Roosevelt set up the WPA, which created all these public projects that gave people jobs. Men wanted to work, so having someplace to work meant so much to them. The jobs weren't much, but it helped families survive. I liken it to people coming across the Mexican border, a daily event here in El Paso. They are just like most people on this side of the border and they are willing to do whatever it takes to support themselves and their families. I don't understand why more Americans can't understand that. We aren't very different. It's just there is a river between us that says we are.

I suppose, looking back, my childhood is one reason why I have always related well to people of all kinds. Back in the 1950s and '60s, and even today, a lot of whites didn't feel comfortable around blacks and Hispanics, especially poor ones. Later, when I would go recruiting as a college basketball coach we'd go into some of the most depressed neighborhoods in America—real tough, troubled spots—but I was always comfortable. I'd sit in tiny apartments on broken couches, even the floor sometimes, and talk to players, moms, and dads like it was no big thing, because, to me, it was no big thing. Sometimes we'd eat real simple, humble meals, and I loved it. When you grow up hunting for dinner and knowing people that were truly poor like I did, that stuff will never bother you. Who was I to look down on anyone? Pinto beans and cornbread for dinner was like reliving my childhood.

The first paying job I ever had was at a feed store in downtown Enid when I was in high school. The big thing to buy was chicken scratch. This was the mid-1940s so the Depression was over and the war was winding down. I got paid a dollar a day, which seemed like a fortune, so I loved the job. I don't remember who started working there first, but I had a coworker, Herman Carr. We were both fifteen. We both loved sports. We were both strong and athletic. We became fast friends, which normally wouldn't have been a big deal except for one thing—Herman Carr was black.

I suppose it is all a matter of perception—and mine being white probably isn't the right one to go by—but I don't recall a lot of overt racism in Enid back then. There weren't any

lynchings or anything violent like that, but the town was segregated. Enid had about twenty-five thousand residents and
out in that part of Oklahoma there wasn't another town for
miles. This was the Great Plains. We had a lot of sky, good
sunsets, but not many people. Enid was in many ways a self-
contained place. You pretty much knew everyone, at least
everyone who was white. The blacks stayed on the other side
of town. You rarely saw a black person at Sanford's Drug-Store,
the main burger-and-Coke place downtown. Blacks couldn't
attend Enid High School; they went to Booker T. Washington
High. There were the water fountains—one for whites, one
for "colored." I remember being about thirteen and seeing a
black soldier from Vance Air Force base in full uniform have
to use the colored fountain and thinking, He's good enough
to get his ass shot for his country, but not to drink out of a
fountain? That bothered me and stuck with me. But I didn't
do anything about it because that's just the way it was. As
dumb as it sounds now, people just accepted it because it was
just the way it had always been.

While all of this is clearly racist, people didn't disapprove
of me and Herman becoming friends. It was a bit unusual,
but no one frowned upon it. Our friendship started at work.
We quickly had contests to see who could lift more hundred-
pound sacks, and then we'd wind up wrestling or whatever.
We just had a good time. For a while there I was better at
baseball than basketball—I was a pitcher and went on to play
some semipro ball. But I always loved basketball, for whatever
reason it was just my favorite sport to play. Oklahoma is foot-

ball country first, then comes baseball (think Mickey Mantle). So getting a great basketball game going wasn't always easy. But Herman loved basketball as much as I did and he was good, real good. We started playing one-on-one after work at the park just off the center of town.

I wasn't a naturally great basketball player. I made the team as a ninth grader, but I didn't do much. I couldn't shoot a free throw to save my life. I was like Shaq, except I wasn't seven foot one. I tried one-handed, two-handed, even under-handed. Nothing worked. But I was determined to get better and I wound up becoming a great shooter because of my dad. Behind our house he had put up a hoop, but it wasn't a traditional-sized hoop. It was much smaller, like the kind they have at the carnival to try to con you into playing. You figure you can hit a ten-footer and win your girlfriend a big teddy bear or some crap like that, but little do you know the rim is only a little bit bigger than the ball. I hated that rim in our yard because it was so hard to hit shots on, but my dad told me that if I could learn to shoot on it then in regular games it would be easy. Maybe he should have been a coach because that system worked. By the time I got to high school the regulation-sized hoop was like a big tub. I could just throw it in there.

The other man who helped my game was my coach, Dale Holt, one of the finest men I ever met. He really worked with me on my shot and got me into basketball. The patience he displayed has always stuck with me. When I became a college coach I didn't just obsess about recruiting better players, I obsessed about working with guys and making them better. I think this is a lost art in college coaching. Now it is just recruit, recruit, recruit. Not teach, teach, teach.

A lot of old guys like me complain about how the fundamentals in sports have been lost and the games are a lot sloppier. A lot of people blame it on kids today being distracted with video games and all of that. But I don't know. I think we are just forgetting that there were plenty of distractions back when I was a kid too. Drinking beer and chasing girls aren't new and have always been popular. Nothing has ruined more jump shots than beer and girls. Personally, I wasn't too interested in girls in those days. I didn't have much time for them. As for beer, one time a couple guys back from the navy got me to have a Blatz beer—peer pressure—and my mother caught me. The endless lectures I got from her for that steered me clear for a while.

I was so into sports and nothing else seemed important to me. They held the Enid High junior/senior prom at the convention hall downtown where we played our high school games. Since we didn't have enough students to fill the whole gym, they hung this big, old curtain down the middle to divide it. Half was enough for us. While the prom goers danced on one side of the curtain, I was shooting baskets on the other side all by myself. They were dancing and having a good time and I was practicing. I was the only one. I was doing what I wanted to do and they were doing what they wanted to do. I don't think they knew I was over there or everyone probably would have laughed their asses off, but I did not want to be on the other side. Everyone chuckles at the story now and sports writers used to love to write about it, but at the time, I'll tell you, I thought everyone on the other side of the curtain was nuts, not me.

During that first summer of high school I was working with Herman, he and I played all the time and I learned immediately that while I could outshoot him, he could not only outjump and outrun me, but outthink me on the court. He was a great player. Herman started for Washington High and had a lot more experience, so he made me better. Not surprisingly, because of all that practicing I got good enough as a sophomore that I became a starter at Enid High. Guys never spent the time I did practicing. They were screwing around, doing whatever. I had been playing three or four hours a day, either with Herman at the park or the gym or behind my house on that carnival rim. Eventually I got written up in the local newspaper and talked about on the local radio. In small towns like Enid, where there isn't much sports other than the local high school, the team becomes the focal point of the town. It was a lot like the movie *Hoosiers*. And since we won a lot of games my junior and senior year, I was a big star in that small pond.

One of the most memorable games that I ever played was during my senior year in the regional playoffs of the state tournament. We were playing Stillwater High School. We won the opening tip, but I missed the shot. We settled into a zone defense. The Stillwater coach didn't want to play against a zone so he instructed his team to hold the ball until we came out of the zone. Well, Coach Holt wasn't going to let another coach dictate the way he played defense, so we stayed in the zone. After a couple minutes of just standing there, the Stillwater point guard put down the ball and sat right on top of it. Then his teammates all sat down on the floor too. So then we sat down. And as the clock ran, all ten players on the floor were just sitting there staring at one another. The first quarter ended that way, score 0–0. At the beginning of the second quarter, we jumped it up and they got the ball. We went right back to the zone and soon everyone was sitting on the floor again. The crowd was hooting and hollering, but no one would move. I hope they didn't pay much to get into the game because this was easily the most boring half of basketball ever played. Sure enough, the clock ran out on the half and the score was 0–0. The guys on the team were cracking jokes in the locker room about how Coach should be proud of our defense considering we had not only shut out Stillwater, but they didn't even manage a single shot.

Second half started and again we won the tip. And again I missed my shot. Unbelievable. And then it all started again. We stay in the zone and they sat down. Score after three quarters, 0–0. Now, at this point, we were all wondering what will happen in the end. I was cursing myself for missing those shots and since I was sitting on the floor I had plenty of time to think. Stillwater won the tip in the fourth and we lined back up in the zone. Everyone was standing around and finally Coach Holt gave in and told us to go play man-to-man. We each got a few baskets and with time running down the score was tied something like 13–13 and Stillwater had the ball. They took a shot to win, but it missed and I grabbed the rebound at the top of the key. The buzzer was about to go off so I spun around and threw the ball one-handed all the way down the floor—about seventy feet. The ball had so much spin on it, it sort of curved as it headed for the rim. And just as the buzzer went off, it goes in—a perfect swish. It went in there so hot it damn near ripped the net off. It was a shot you couldn't make if you had fifty tries but bang, there it is. Final score Enid 15, Stillwater 13. We went crazy. This was the most bizarre game I had ever seen. It wasn't funny to Stillwater though. Their coach actually had a heart attack and had to be rushed to the hospital (he survived). This game was the highpoint of my high school career, especially since we were eliminated in the state tournament soon after.

I was named all-state as a senior and some people were claiming I was an All-American. I never really understood how one could figure I was an All-American when I hadn't even played all the other kids in Oklahoma. But it didn't matter, the recognition was enough for me to get over one hundred scholarship offers to college. This was probably the first time I thought about how race affected people. I remember looking at all of these scholarship offers, the all-state awards, the stories in the newspaper, and thinking, I don't deserve these. Some people were saying that I was the best player in all of Oklahoma and the reality was, I wasn't even the best player in Enid. Herman Carr was. But because he went to Washington High, the newspapers barely wrote about him.

Reporters didn't even cover the Washington games. There would just be this little write-up in the corner of an inside page, "Herman Carr scored twenty-seven points . . ." A couple of paragraphs and that was it.

No one named him all-state and no colleges came to recruit him because he was black. This was in 1948. It was as if he didn't even exist. I thought this was terribly unfair and I felt bad for my friend. I had no idea how this could happen. Herman was plenty smart enough to go to college. I knew that. He would have been great for Oklahoma A&M, but he was never even considered. I can't say I did anything about it, but I knew it was wrong and it stuck in the back of my mind. It turns out Herman joined the Army so he could keep playing basketball. How about that? The Army was the only place in America a black kid could keep playing basketball. Fair? Bullshit. Herman and I lost touch after high school for a while, but later in life we got back in touch with each other and now talk on the phone every so often. It is a friendship I really value, because he taught me a lot of things about life in America that white kids just didn't learn back in those days.

While I had no lack of college offers, most of the recruiters were wasting their time. I was an Oklahoma A&M (now Oklahoma State) fan growing up. Under Mr. Henry Iba the Aggies had won the 1945 and 1946 national titles and I had gotten hooked on them. I used to lie in my bedroom and listen to their games on KBOO out of Tulsa, Oklahoma. John Henry, and later Kurt Gowdy, was the voice of the Aggies. A&M was always one of the top teams in the country and everyone wanted to play for them. The team was so popular Gallagher Hall was sold out every night.

Bruce Drake was the coach at the University of Oklahoma and he came to try to recruit me. One day Drake was sitting out in front of Enid High School in a big old Oldsmobile. It was a real fancy car but it had a dent in it. I came outside after school and he told me that the dent was caused by one of his players. He had let the guy borrow the car to use on a date the other night and he dented the car. He knew I was leaning toward Oklahoma A&M so he told me, "Don, I want you to go over to Oklahoma A&M and ask if when you are a player you can borrow Henry's car."

First, it was funny that Drake called him Henry. Nobody dared call Mr. Iba "Henry," even when he wasn't around. To this day, and Mr. Iba died in 1993, you'll never hear any of his former players call him Henry. It is Mr. Iba or Coach Iba. Well, I didn't even understand the joke about borrowing Mr. Iba's car until after about a week into my freshman year at Oklahoma A&M. Mr. Iba was the meanest son of a gun you ever met. I can't even imagine anyone having the courage even to ask to borrow Mr. Iba's car for a date. If you did, he probably would have kicked your ass just for thinking it. We didn't even dare tell him we liked girls. Once I became a player for Mr. Iba I thought back to that day Drake had pulled up in front of Enid High and I just started cracking up. I thought, Dang, Bruce Drake was right; I ain't going to be borrowing this man's car.

A lot of fans think that cheating in college sports is worse than ever or that it is some new thing. Forget it. There has been cheating in college sports for as long as there have been alumni who cared who won. The NCAA has all sorts of rules and all sorts of investigators whose job it is to punish the schools who do it, but it has never been able to stop it and never will. I had some offers for payouts, including one offer I strongly considered. At the time my mother was ill—she had a gallbladder problem. She needed an operation, but we didn't have the money for anything like that. Well, a school offered me three thousand dollars for the operation if I would play for them. They also said I could make a hundred dollars a month while I was there and all I had to do was "wind the clock" on campus, basically a no-show, nothing-to-do job. Well, I took that offer to my parents because it was a lot of money. My mother told me that in no way, shape, or form would she accept any money for me to go to college. She didn't want any "wind the clock" handouts. She wanted me to go wherever I wanted to go. My dad agreed. So that was that.

In reality, I was always going to go to Oklahoma A&M and I knew it. Coach Holt did not want me to go to Oklahoma A&M because I was a shooter and Mr. Iba was all about defense. He didn't let guys shoot much. Coach Holt thought I would have been a better player if I went to the University of Oklahoma because they played a freer offensive system. Coach Holt was probably right but I wasn't interested in listening to reason; I was in awe of Mr. Iba.

To seal the deal, Mr. Iba came to Enid to meet with me. This was a big thing because Mr. Iba almost never made a recruiting visit. Although we lived just a little more than an hour from campus, it was huge when he came to my house with his assistant. To Enid this was bigger than the governor visiting. This is how much Mr. Iba meant to small towns in Oklahoma. We didn't have a whole lot out there then to be proud of and usually people around the country thought of Okies as rednecks who didn't leave during the Dust Bowl. So when Mr. Iba gave us those two national titles, he made us proud and showed the nation that something positive can come out of Oklahoma.

The day he came to Enid to recruit me I pitched a baseball game in the afternoon. He came to the ballpark to watch. The whole place was buzzing, people were going up to him and getting autographs. Afterwards, he came to my house and talked to my parents. During the whole meeting he never mentioned basketball. He talked about education and all of the other benefits of college. He never talked about how good of a player I was, like the other recruiters had. And he didn't offer any money or no-show jobs. My parents loved it. He was a charmer. They ate it up. When he left I knew where I was going. I was going to be an Aggie.

THREE

OKLAHOMA A&M

"So how was being an Aggie?" I asked Haskins.

This was one of our first interviews, back in 1997 when he was still the coach of UTEP, obsessed about how his players weren't getting back on defense, and I was a reporter, bothering him in the middle of the season. We were at a Holiday Inn in El Paso getting breakfast; Haskins, fresh from a heart ailment, was having Raisin Bran. It was so unappealing to him, what with his favorite, huevos rancheros, on the menu, he basically stirred it around in protest.

He stopped at my question and looked at me like it was a silly inquiry. We barely knew each other. I thought, at first, that he thought I was being a wise guy making fun of him, because, face it, the prospect of being an Aggie isn't really something that most kids from the North go to sleep dreaming of becoming.

But he didn't think that. He was just surprised that I had no idea of what being an Aggie under Mr. Iba really meant. Throughout the Great Plains, Iba and his coaching tactics are legendary. Elsewhere, however, Iba isn't as famous.

In advance of the interview I had spoken to a number of Haskins's former players, who regaled me with stories of six-hour practices, no water breaks, and endless sprints. They spoke of the coach's single-minded focus, volatile temper, and seemingly strange rules. One of his first players, Steve Tredennick, told me that Haskins was so against the idea of players having girlfriends that after games Tredennick's future wife would hide behind the bleachers to meet him so Haskins wouldn't find out they were dating.

But while everyone agreed Haskins was a hard-driving, occasionally brutal coach who they intensely disliked during their playing days, once they graduated they came to cherish the toughness and discipline he had instilled in them. They marveled at how he became the most loyal friend they would ever know.

"I hated him when I was there," said Nevil Shed, a player on his 1966 championship team. "God knows I hated that man. But for what he's done for me since I graduated, I wouldn't trade it for anything. He is a great, great man. He is the best thing ever to happen to me."

That day at the Holiday Inn, I learned where Haskins's coaching personality was shaped. I heard where the idea of iron discipline, endless practice, and unconditional loyalty came from.

"What was it like being an Aggie?" I had asked.
Haskins looked up from his Raisin Bran and finally answered.
"Ever have the ball of your foot fall off?"

■

Playing for Mr. Iba was four years of hell. Four years of hell I wouldn't trade for the world. I know that sounds ridiculous. And it sounds self-centered because, really, how bad could going to college for free and playing basketball be? It was the opportunity of a lifetime for a kid from Dust Bowl Enid. And I understood all of that, even at the time.

If you know what it was like playing for Mr. Iba, then you wouldn't think I was crazy for calling it hell. And just about every other guy who ever played for him says the exact same thing. When you were there it couldn't have been worse. But when it was over, it couldn't have been better. Mr. Iba barely spoke to you (although he did yell a lot) when you were a player. But once you graduated he was your best friend; he'd do anything for you. Once you paid your debt to him, he spent the rest of his life paying you back, only tenfold. As I look back, I realize that just about every good thing that ever happened to me in my life is a result of playing for Mr. Iba. Not just the connections from being part of his inner circle, but the lessons he taught. The way he showed us how to conduct business, treat people, work hard, and stay focused was invaluable. Especially for someone who went on to be a college basketball coach. Mr. Iba was the greatest, most innovative coach who ever lived. And I learned from him. You don't think that helped me later as a coach?

But when I was eighteen and didn't know what I know now, I hated it. I hated every minute of playing for him. I even hated him. I tried to quit every day for four years, but I was just too afraid of Mr. Iba to tell him. I tried to transfer. If I played well in a game I would write a letter to the other coach saying I wanted to transfer to his school. None ever wrote back. I think they were scared of Mr. Iba too. I kept trying. I'd go to sleep at night cursing myself for not going to the University of Oklahoma, where I would have been able to shoot the ball anytime I wanted, and then borrow Bruce Drake's big Oldsmobile for dates on the weekends. I know what follows will sound like old, inflated war stories, the kind old people always tell—"I had to walk uphill to school, both ways . . ."—but they are all true. Ask anyone who played for Mr. Iba. I remember once a guy a couple years older than I, who I had played with, had graduated and come back to campus when I was a senior. He had joined the Marines right after graduation and was on leave or something. I said, "Bob, what are the Marines like?" He said, "After four years of Mr. Iba, a piece of cake."

Henry Iba was known as the Iron Duke and I can't think of a nickname that was more appropriate. He was about six foot two, fit as can be his entire life, and always perfectly groomed, his hair combed exactly. The man always looked perfect. My high school coach, Coach Holt, was right about my style of play not fitting in at A&M. I was a shooter and Mr. Iba liked to control every play. In high school if I missed five shots, Coach Holt would say, "Keep shooting, you'll make the next five." Well, I damn sure never heard that in Stillwater, I can assure you that. In that day and age, all college coaches, such as Phog Allen at Kansas or Jack Hartman at Kansas State, were controlling, so it wasn't just Mr. Iba, but I think he took it to another level. Mr. Iba had led Oklahoma A&M to back-to-back national championships in 1945 and 1946 when he had a seven-footer named Bob Kurland. That made Mr. Iba a legend in Oklahoma, one of the most powerful people in the entire state. So Mr. Iba not only believed in being completely in charge of all encounters, especially with players, but he had the success to demand it.

Almost everyone has heard of Bear Bryant's Junction Boys, his first football team at Texas A&M that he took to Junction, Texas, and practiced so hard that just about all of them quit. Well, Mr. Iba was the basketball version of Bear Bryant. Same era, same part of the country, same mind-set. In four years of practice I said two words. One time I said, "I thought . . ." and Mr. Iba heard me and the tirade began. "Haskins, you haven't had a thought in your mind your entire life. If you ever have another thought again on my time, you better not express it." And so on. That was how it was. Nowadays the NCAA has rules saying a team can't practice more than twenty hours a week when school is in session. A coach can't start holding practice until October 15 and is required to give players at least one day off a week. There were no such rules back when Mr. Iba coached. We practiced all year round. No summer vacation. On nonschool days we'd go three times a day, nine hours total. I am serious. It would get so hot in the summer you'd just sweat and sweat. One year I went from one hundred eighty pounds to one hundred sixty. I was six foot one. Damn, were we skinny.

On days with no class, we'd start practice at 9:00 A.M. sharp and go until noon, then 2:00 P.M. to 5:00 P.M. and then, finally, 7:00 P.M. to 10:00 P.M. All we'd do is practice. Going to play games was a damn joke because physically it was far less demanding than practice. Mr. Iba was big on fundamentals and defense. He was easily the greatest defensive coach of all time. We worked over and over on man-to-man defense (he didn't believe in zones) and then worked on set plays, but mainly it was defense and toughness. He valued each possession like it was his firstborn. If you shot and missed, you caught some serious hell. Even in practice. I remember missing a couple jumpers once in practice and Mr. Iba went nuts on me. He said, "You've been standing over there in the cool breeze shooting them long jumpers and them poor other guys are under the basket getting knots on their head." He'd say things like that, stuff that was really funny. He had a hell of a sense of humor, but the only thing was, none of us dared laugh.

Under Mr. Iba, there was no sitting during practice. When you weren't in a drill or a scrimmage you stood. There was also no water. Coaches during that time didn't believe in water breaks. Not Bear Bryant, not Iba, not lots of coaches.

They thought it slowed players down and gave them cramps. We also were never allowed to eat ketchup. Mr. Iba was convinced ketchup hurt your wind. After games we had to eat cereal and ice cream because it supposedly helped you to recover. I know this sounds stupid now, but that was how it was. And let me tell you, when I became coach at Texas Western I didn't allow water breaks for years. Eventually I did, around the late 1970s, and when my old players would come back to watch practice and see guys drinking water, they'd say, "Hey, what's that? You getting soft?"

The one thing about being tough is that it always instills togetherness among the players. It is no different than how the military runs boot camp. You make it so hard on them, you make them hate you so much, that they don't have the time or energy to turn on each other—sort of a band of brothers against the old bastard. That is how it was for us. The players were best friends because all our hate was directed at Mr. Iba. And he liked it that way.

Practicing for Coach Iba was tough enough on days when he wasn't mad at you, but when he was, well, damn, forget it. And since I was a smart aleck back then, guess who he was mad at a lot? Every so often he'd get on a guy and ride him the whole day, just brutalize him, scream at him, pick on him. God, you'd feel sorry for that bastard, but it was effective. You could do nothing right on those days. One day during Christmas break my sophomore year, I was "that guy." He was on my ass for something and he started in on me right away, right at 9:00 A.M. We were going through a set play on offense and I was supposed to run to an exact spot and catch a pass. I did it perfectly, exactly as he had showed me, and I knew it. But he started screaming at me, "Haskins, you knucklehead." And I am thinking, What could I have done wrong? He ran over and pointed at the board on the floor that is right next to my foot, about half an inch from where I was. "This board. This is the board you are supposed to be on, not that one." It was crazy, but it made everyone acutely aware that you were one small screwup away from being "that guy" at practice.

I don't remember why, although I probably deserved it, but shortly after came my day in the hole. No getting out of a drill, no getting off the floor, no rest. If there was something happening, I was in it. Everyone else would rotate in and out but not me. We scrimmaged for three hours in the morning, and by the end I was exhausted. We did three more hours in the afternoon and by the end I could feel the balls of my feet moving. I used to have these huge blisters back then, so I was used to some of it, but this time it felt different. Every time I planted my foot it felt like I might just slide off the ball of my foot. We scrimmaged again in the evening and I was in so much pain after the first hour. But I couldn't show it. One, I didn't want to give that bastard any satisfaction and two, it would only make him work me harder. We had about a one-minute break after the first hour while Mr. Iba reorganized what he wanted to do. I was physically whipped and I thought Mr. Iba would take me out. But hell no. He ran me the second and third hour too. Nine hours of scrimmaging.

This is the type of behavior that could get a coach fired

now. Hell, maybe even locked up. But not then. I never thought of doing something chickenshit like complain to a school official—I was taught to take it like a man and I did, everyone did—but even if I had, it wouldn't have done much good. Mr. Iba had the full control and full support of everyone in the administration. He was the most powerful person at Oklahoma A&M.

When that practice finally ended that night I walked off the court on the sides of my feet. I couldn't put any pressure on the balls of my feet. The president of the school was there, Dr. Bennett. He was Mr. Iba's friend. He looked at me and said, "Son, are your feet sore?" And I said, "No sir." And he said, "Good, they shouldn't be because you haven't done a damn thing all day." The president of the school! This is how things were back then. I got into the training room and took off my sock. The ball of my foot just fell off. The fat part came completely off. I got a bunch of tape from the trainer, taped it back on, and was ready to go the next day. I may have hated Mr. Iba, but I wasn't going to let him break me. This is just how kids were back in Oklahoma in the 1940s and '50s.

After college Mr. Iba and I became great, great friends. I consider him the greatest man I ever met. I never stopped admiring his discipline, his intelligence, and his leadership abilities. This is a man who could have been a success in any field he had tried, business, the military, whatever. Obviously, as an adult, he no longer had the power to make my foot fall off, but even still, there was never a time I wasn't still a little afraid of him.

Mr. Iba was the U.S. Olympic coach three times. He won two gold medals and I was his assistant on the famous 1972 team that lost the gold medal game to the Soviet Union when some corrupt officiating screwed us over. I was forty-two years old in 1972, I had won a national championship myself at Texas Western, had four children, and was a successful guy. But I was still scared of him. We trained the Olympic team that summer out in Colorado Springs. I got Mr. Iba to let my friend Bob Knight, who was then just hired as head coach at Indiana, to work as a volunteer assistant. Knight, get this, would be the referee during scrimmages, he even donned a referee shirt (damn, what I would give for a picture of that). Well, one night during this time we are out at a bar in Colorado Springs and Knight says to me, "All you former A&M guys are always so afraid of Mr. Iba." And I said, "Shit, Bob, you would be too if your foot ever fell off." I suspect it is the same way now with Knight and his former players. No matter how old and successful a player gets, there is still a little bit of fear there for his former coach.

We played every year in the All-College Tournament in Oklahoma City, which was a big deal back then and featured eight top teams from around the country. Mr. Iba was easier on us on game days in order to save our legs a bit, but easier wasn't the same as easy. We were set to play at 7:30 P.M. my sophomore year but we were already at the gym in Oklahoma City by 1:00 P.M. He told us to go out and "shoot a little," which meant that we start scrimmaging. Mr. Iba drove us hard and four hours later we were still going. By this point the two teams who are scheduled to play in the consolation game at 5:00 P.M. have shown up and there are fans in the stands. And Mr. Iba is going nuts anyway, yelling and everything. People are shocked. Finally, the tournament director works up the courage to tell Mr. Iba his scrimmage has to end because the consolation game has to begin. Mr. Iba was furious we were being run off the floor. We wound up winning the tournament final that night, but only because we were too afraid to lose.

It wasn't all about basketball though at A&M, although it certainly dominated my life. There wasn't much to Stillwater then and the school had only about twelve thousand students. When I was a freshman I met a girl named Mary Gorman of Midwest City, Oklahoma. I didn't do a lot of dating, but somehow I had a date with one of her sorority sisters and that was how I met Mary. We hit it off right away and that was all she wrote for the sorority sister. Mary was pretty and smart and I was very interested in her. We dated for about a year and then we got married before my sophomore year. That's how a lot of guys did it back then. There were a lot more military veterans in college, so they were older, and in general people just got married sooner.

We had our first son, Mark, while I was a senior in college and moved into married student housing. Getting married also got Mr. Iba off your back. He didn't care much for girlfriends, but he loved wives. It was the damnedest thing. I have no idea how he thought we could get a wife without having a girlfriend, but I didn't have the courage to ask. All I knew was he hated, hated girlfriends. He thought they were bad for your wind, so we learned quickly never to let Mr. Iba catch you with a girl. And when I mean catch, I mean even talking to one about a term paper in the middle of campus at noon on a Tuesday.

I remember one time we were about to catch a bus for some road trip. My teammate Bob Seymour and I were there early so we went across the street to grab a Coke. As we came out we saw another teammate, Keith Smith, walking toward the bus holding hands with his girlfriend. Right then we see Mr. Iba's big green Oldsmobile turn the corner and he sees Smith and this hand-holding session. The girl sees Mr. Iba's car and immediately veers off, disappears like she wasn't even there, and Keith keeps walking, never breaking stride. But Bob and I are laughing inside because we know Mr. Iba saw it and ole Keith is in for it. God knows what he was thinking, holding hands with a girl in a place where Mr. Iba is likely to see him. Everyone got on the bus and Mr. Iba starts laying into Keith for fifteen minutes for this hand-holding session with his girlfriend. He didn't play Keith the next night. The guy got benched for holding hands.

I was on my best behavior, for the most part, at Oklahoma A&M. This was because Mr. Iba had the whole town wired. You couldn't do anything without him knowing about it. I remember one day I joined a fraternity. I didn't even want to join but this guy was hounding me. The fraternities always wanted athletes to join. So one afternoon I joined. But that night some guy demanded I shine his shoes and I quit on the spot. I was part of the fraternity for about six hours. The next day I get called into Mr. Iba's office. He hated fraternities. He called them lodges. And he said, "I heard you joined a lodge." I said, "I already quit." He yelled at me anyway. His pipeline in Stillwater was uncanny. One thing you didn't do was go out in town. After a victory some of our guys went to a bar called the Rock Inn for a couple beers. I didn't do it; I was home with Mary and Mark. But that was the biggest mistake they ever made. The next four days what Mr. Iba did to those guys was inhumane. Just unbelievable. And all four of them were Army veterans. They were in their mid-twenties, married, good guys. It didn't make any difference to Mr. Iba.

We played our games at the university's gym, Gallagher Hall, which when it was built in 1930 was heralded as the Madison Square Garden of the Plains. Later when I traveled to New York, I found this funny. Not that Gallagher Hall—they later added Mr. Iba's name to it so it is now referred to as Gallagher-Iba Arena—isn't a great arena. But the middle of the Oklahoma A&M campus isn't often confused or compared to midtown Manhattan. I'll tell you what Gallagher Hall was, though: the loudest arena in the country. It seated about eight thousand when I was a player (it seats over thirteen thousand now), everyone dressed in orange and they brought a cowbell to ring. This was before the NCAA banned noisemakers from games. People have said Gallagher-Iba is the loudest gym in the country now, so can you imagine how loud it was when eight thousand people were ringing cowbells?

We had some great teams back then, great games. At the time we were in the Missouri Valley Conference and the rules were that only one team from each conference would go to the NCAA tournament. Our team was always ranked in the top five and Bradley or St. Louis would also rank in the top ten. So we played some big games. Mr. Iba would get keyed up for only two or three games a season and one of them was against St. Louis and its coach Ed Hickey. He and Mr. Iba hated each other. I don't know why, but Mr. Iba made sure we knew this game was important. Ed Hickey was about five foot five and had a shiny bald head. It was always, "Eddie this, Eddie that" the week before the game. So everyone on the team knew how much a game against St. Louis meant to Mr. Iba. One year we played in Kiel Auditorium in St. Louis for the Missouri Valley Championship. It was always wild when we played there. The fans were crazy and it was obvious that the St. Louis players knew Ed Hickey didn't like Mr. Iba any more than Mr. Iba liked Ed Hickey. This game meant everything. Both teams knew if we lost the game our coach was going to put us through hell. So it wasn't so much winning the game for our coach—truth was, both teams hated their coaches—it was a matter of damn survival. Screw up in this one and you were going to get it in practice.

It was this game during my sophomore year when I was out on the floor and something happened at the scorer's table. Mr. Iba started to walk down to the table. Eddie Hickey saw this and he charged down there too. They met up at the scorer's table and started getting into it. I was standing out at midcourt, we didn't know what was happening, but it was funny. Mr. Iba was staring straight down at Hickey. Mr. Iba's face was fiery red and his hands behind his back, clasped. Then all of a sudden Hickey put his dukes up for some reason. It looked like they were about to fight. You could tell the players hated their coaches because no one moved to break it up. We just all stood there, waiting to see what would happen. A kid from St. Louis was standing next to me and he said, "I hope Iba knocks the shit out of him." And I started laughing and said, "I hope Hickey gets one in on Iba." It turns out no one threw a punch, they just cussed out each other for a while, but now it was clear we absolutely had to win even more than before the argument. If not, we were sure one of us was going to lose the ball of a foot.

Near the end of the game, we were down a point. I had the ball with about three seconds remaining. The plan was to get the ball to our center, Bob Maddox. We also had this big ole blond-headed sophomore by the name of Bob Hendricks, who Mr. Iba called the Wild Man. And he *was* wild as hell. He was always going too fast, playing out of control. He was a great athlete, but he would take these crazy shots; you never knew what was going to happen. He'd either do something spectacular or throw it over the backboard. For Mr. Iba, who liked to control everything, this was unacceptable. Hendricks was a sophomore and the only reason he was in the game was because someone had fouled out. Otherwise Mr. Iba wouldn't have trusted him to bring him a cup of water.

So I had the ball and the play was for Maddox, who was

down by the post, but covered a little bit. For some reason, Hendricks came running around a screen, a curl, as you'd call it today, and he was wide open. I mean *wide* open. I don't know why I threw it to the Wild Man but I did. Hendricks got it, hooked it in off the backboard so hard it almost broke the glass. Total cannonball shot. But it hit the glass—*wham*—and then it went in. Buzzer sounded, we won the Missouri Valley Championship. This was always the maddening, funny thing about Coach Iba. I caught hell all the way to the locker room. Was he glad we won the game? Hell no. He charges out on the court and starts screaming in my ear. "Haskins, you are crazy. The Wild Man? How could you throw it to the Wild Man?" He chews my ass all the way to the locker room for throwing the ball to Hendricks. I actually think he would have rather lost the game than have seen me throw it to the Wild Man.

I played three years of varsity basketball at Oklahoma A&M (freshmen could play only on the freshman team then), often as a reserve. I had some moments, but I was never a star. It seemed like every time I started believing in myself I would lose confidence. My sophomore year we played in the big All-College Tournament in Oklahoma City. I made the all-star team for the event. I thought I was onto something, but then Mr. Iba benched me for the next three games. I never even got in. Can you imagine that happening now? The press would be going crazy, the kid would probably transfer on the spot. But not back then. I didn't know why I was benched and I didn't dare ask.

Finally, in 1972 when Mr. Iba and I were in Munich, Germany, for the Olympics, the two of us went out and got to drinking a bit. He had a little of the Old Crow whiskey in him and I had some tequila and I finally had the courage to ask.

I said, "Mr. Iba, how come after I made the All-College Tournament team as a sophomore you benched me for those three games?" And he paused for a second and said, "I thought you might be getting a little chesty."

Chesty? Now that's funny. The only time in my college career I felt the least bit confident and he figured I had become arrogant and needed to be taken down a couple of pegs. That was playing for Mr. Iba though; the four worst and four best years of my life.

TUMBLEWEED HIGH

"Had a big weekend," Haskins bragged through the phone, a hint of humor in his voice. It was early on a Monday, just 7:00 A.M. That's Haskins. He calls early. I live in the Eastern Time Zone, he lives in the Mountain Time Zone. And he stills manages to call early.

"Really, and what exactly constitutes a big weekend?" I asked a man who by this point, in 2003, was retired and could go years without leaving El Paso.

"Gave a speech to a high school graduating class," he said.

I didn't believe it. Despite living a public life, Haskins is shy.

One of the reasons he stayed at UTEP, rather than go to a big school somewhere, is that he is wary of the press, especially in big numbers. He wasn't much for booster lunches or alumni functions. UTEP didn't make him do stuff like that. The limelight just isn't for him. He knew he wouldn't be so lucky in the Big Twelve.

The reality was other than talking to his team he didn't like addressing a crowd of even five people—unless they were all leaning on a brass rail in a bar, of course.

So a speech to a high school graduating class? This sounded unlikely.

"What high school?"

"Benjamin High School."

This was going to be good.

"They had a baby boom since I was there. Sign at the edge of town said population two hundred and fifty-three."

I laughed. "So how many young graduates were there to soak up your wisdom?"

"Four."

■

After four years at Oklahoma A&M I was out of NCAA eligibility. Notice I didn't say I actually graduated from the place. Like a lot of college basketball players, after four years on campus, I hadn't earned a degree. Looking back on it, I was one stupid ole boy. I know that. How could you be given such an opportunity—a free education—and not take full advantage of it? It's been over fifty years and I still haven't thought up a good answer. I've spent a lot of time kicking myself for not gettin' it done, trust me. I think this is why I used to harp on my players so much about earning that degree. You can ask any of them, I said it so often they plumb got sick of hearing it. I knew firsthand the mistake they would be making. I didn't want them making it too.

I was twelve credits short of a degree. Looking back, I think my main problem was shooting pool. I was always missing class because I spent more time in the pool hall than the lecture hall. You know that old deal, I missed Monday but I'll go Wednesday. I'll go next time. Yeah, right. I never dared miss practice, of course, but class was different.

I was done with college, but had no piece of paper. I could still play professional ball, the question was where? The NBA was just starting out and it was mainly in the East, but there was Amateur Athletic Union (AAU) basketball, which gave me a couple of options. This was during a time when companies sponsored teams—the Akron Firestone Non-Skids, the Peoria Caterpillar Cats, the Phillips 66ers out of Bartlesville, Oklahoma—in an effort to promote their product and build morale. While it doesn't compare to life as a modern NBA star, the players would get jobs with the company and then play ball. Being as young as I was, it felt like the Life of Riley.

I wound up with the Artesia (N.M.) Travelers, which was sponsored by a power company. My job was to go out in the desert and check the power lines. But we players had contests to see who could do less work. We were only there to play ball and we knew it. After four years of playing under the heavy hand of Mr. Iba, AAU ball was a blast. All we did was shoot. No defense. I had a game where I scored thirty-eight points against the Denver Bankers. I never missed a shot, nineteen for nineteen. But while the game was fun to play, it was also frustrating. Our coach was a nice guy, but he had played just a little high school ball. He worked at the company and admitted he didn't know how to coach.

I disliked the way we played. I remember Phillips 66 beating us one night 119 to 116. I went home and thought, Son of a bitch, if we just could get back on defense we could win a lot of games. That's when I started to realize that Mr. Iba knew what he was talking about after all. I once thought he was the dumbest coach in the world. Now he was the smartest.

Mary was working at a bank in Artesia then, but she started putting it on me to get a career, because obviously I couldn't play forever. It wasn't like the NBA today where you earn so much money that when you retire you can just go fishing. Since we already had our first child, Mark, it was time to get on with my life. Mary suggested I get into coaching. She was probably smart enough to know I was too dumb to do anything else. She had been telling me since college that she wanted me to be a coach. The idea never appealed to me, but at this point in my life I didn't have any better ideas.

At Mary's urging I went to a coaches' clinic in Albuquerque and ran into a couple friends of Coach Iba's. George McCarty was there and he was the head coach at Texas Western at the time. He offered me an assistant coaching job with the understanding I could finish my degree. Very few high schools, let alone colleges, would hire a coach or a teacher who didn't have a college degree. So until I got that diploma, my options were limited. I should have taken George up on the offer, but instead another friend of Mr. Iba's, Poke Robinson, said, "I know the superintendent of schools in Benjamin and he needs a head coach and he doesn't care if you have your degree."

I had no idea what (or who) Benjamin was, but it interested me because I figured with all the experience I had I should be a head coach, not an assistant. So Poke went over to this pay phone and called the superintendent of the school, D.V. Markham. When I say superintendent of the school I mean school. Not "schools," as in plural. One school. One building. For the whole town. After about a minute, Poke waved me over to speak to Mr. Markham. We asked each other a couple of questions and then I took the job. It would pay $28,000 per year. I hadn't seen Benjamin and Markham hadn't seen me. I didn't have a degree and he didn't care. He said while I couldn't teach without a degree, I could drive the school bus (an extra four hundred dollars) and coach. If I had any sense in me I would have stopped to think about why a school was hiring a guy they knew nothing about, sight unseen, who had no degree and no coaching experience. But I didn't.

I called home and told Mary about the job of head coach in Benjamin, Texas, and to start packing. I expected her to be proud of me. Instead, she asked me where exactly Benjamin, Texas, was. I told her I had no idea. She got out a map of Texas but couldn't find it. I told her not to worry, it had to be somewhere. God bless her, she didn't even chew my ass out. About a week later I loaded a U-Haul trailer and damn, we almost cried when we pulled up to this little, little town, sort of between Lubbock and Wichita Falls. If you have ever been between Lubbock and Wichita Falls that pretty much says it all. The sign at the edge of town said Benjamin had a population of 230. There was one stoplight and one restaurant.

Over the phone we had arranged to rent a little ole house for thirty-five dollars a month. We pull up on a dirt road and the entire yard was covered with high, overgrown weeds. No other house within a block. No telephone, no mail delivery, nothing. I tried to make the most of it by talking up all the positives, hoping Mary wouldn't make the smart play of stealing the car, hightailing it to her mother's house in Oklahoma, and filing for divorce. I started pulling things from the U-Haul while Mary got Mark out of the car and started up the little walkway. All of a sudden we heard this rattle. Right there on the front stoop was a damn rattlesnake, all coiled up and ready to strike. Almost scared Mary to death. I had a shotgun, so I told her to stay still, got the gun, and went up and killed the snake. Welcome to Benjamin.

I was twenty-four years old then and had never even been an assistant coach, but I wasn't ever nervous about coaching. I was shy then (still am), so about the only thing I ever feared was giving a speech to the Kiwanis Club or something. Fortunately, Benjamin was too small for one of those. But I do admit I was a bit apprehensive that first day of school because I found out I also had to coach six-man football, and I had never even seen a game before. Six-man is how football is played in small towns that don't have enough kids to play a real eleven-on-eleven game. It is a heck of a sport, wide-open, wild, a lot of fun. I always thought they should put it on ESPN sometime. I had played high school football, but this was an entirely new game.

I told Mr. Markham I didn't know anything about six-man football. And he said in that dry, west Texas way, "Well, son, you are going to learn a lot about it then." Gee, thanks. But he sat me down and showed me some things, like cross-blocks and what have you. And that was that, just call me Coach. Of course, I was just dumb enough to go to my first six-man football practice wearing a little blue suede jacket. I was dressed for basketball and tried to look impressive. I think Mary felt sorry for me, it was hotter than hell and dusty out there. I looked ridiculous.

I had nine players and I almost killed them in the first week of practice. It is dry in west Texas and the town wasn't going to waste ranchers' water on a football field, so we played on dirt with old glass on it. I had my guys playing full contact every day, lots of blocking and tackling. I didn't know any better. I figured I needed to toughen them up, Mr. Iba style. That's all I knew, so I acted tough. Hell, Bear Bryant would have loved the Benjamin High six-man football team. One day Mr. Markham comes over, sees all this hitting, almost faints, and says, "Don, in football you can't tackle and block every day." I learned that six-man football is about executing offensive plays, not lining up two-on-two, three-on-three and killing each other.

This was not the last lesson I would learn about the sport. That Friday night we played our first game at Paint Creek. I was all ready, all fired up. It is pretty easy to score in six-man football because there are so few players and so much room. We won the toss and chose to receive the kick. My little guy Johnny Bateman takes it eighty yards and we are in tall cotton. I knew that if you ran the ball in for the extra point you got only one point, not two like in regular football. I remember some of my players mumbling about us practicing kicking extra points, but I kept thinking they were crazy. Why try a kick, which is difficult, when it was so easy to run just two yards and get the point? So we run it in and are up 7 to 0. Then Paint Creek gets the ball and they put a drive together and go in and score a TD. I am angry because I am still thinking like Mr. Iba and I can't stand weak defense. They line up for a kick. I am thinking this other coach is dumber than dumb, some crazy fool. They kick it through and the little scoreboard in the corner says 8 to 7.

I am pissed off now. There was this redheaded official, a tall guy. So I call him over and tell him they got the scoreboard wrong. I yell, "It is seven to seven, not eight to seven." He looked at me and said, "You don't know a hell of a lot about six-man football, do you?" So I immediately take the offensive, I am not going to take any bullshit from this guy. I told him he was a cheating you-know-what and I may be the new guy in the area but I wasn't going to take it. He says nothing, just hands me his little rule book and underlines a couple lines. It says you get one point for running, two points for kicking, since it is harder to do.

I had no idea. That shut me up. It probably was the only time in my career a ref was right. Then we went on to lose the game. My coaching career started with a loss.

It turned out we had a pretty good six-man football team that year. We went on to win the district championship for the first time in school history. You can't even imagine how big of a to-do that was in Benjamin. Just think of some of the big-name towns we used to play: Noodle, Paint Creek, Groom, Quail, Turkey. We were going to play for the bi-district title against McGardle High School and a crowd of about four hundred came to the game, which, if you consider the combined population of the two towns was about six hundred, was considered a pretty impressive turnout. But in small towns life revolves around the high school. Games are big social events because there isn't anything else to do—no bars, movies, malls, whatever. People go to the games just to get out of the house. McGardle beat us that night in a close game and I was ready to kill myself. I can't recall a loss ever hurting more than that. Not in my entire coaching career.

Basketball season was next and I felt more comfortable. I coached both the boys' and the girls' teams and I treated them equal, even though at the time no one else did. Girls' high school sports at the time was basically gym class. But I just coach. To me, they were all just players. I hardly thought about whether they were boys or girls. I just wanted to win. So whatever the boys had to do, the girls had to do. Same drills, same expectations, same sprints. If a girl screwed up, I gave her hell just like I would a boy. I'll tell you something interesting: In all my days of coaching girls I never had one quit. Not one. I had boys quit, but never girls. And if they thought I was tough in football, well, in basketball I was probably even worse. Boy, was I hard on those kids. I drove them, rode them, hollered at them, you name it.

We started winning right away and the town was really excited. But the honeymoon didn't last long because I almost got fired by midseason. We played a little tournament over in Noodle, Texas. My boys got beat 30 to 29, and the girls lost a one pointer to Paint Creek. I was beside myself. I drove the bus home with the girls on one side, the boys on the other. And no talking. There would be no talking or socializing on my time. We got back to Benjamin about 11:00 P.M., but instead of driving the kids home we went to the gym and started practicing. I hated losing so much and I figured we needed to get better, so I thought, Why wait until the next day? I kept them there until 3:00 A.M., giving them all sorts of hell. By that time some parents had shown up and they were angrier than a castrated bull. It was 3:00 A.M. on a school night and their teenage child isn't home. Hell, I don't blame them a bit. But at the time, it made perfect sense to me; there is no time like the present to get better. This was something Mr. Iba would have done to his players, so why shouldn't I do it to mine? I broke up practice and drove the kids whose parents weren't there home on the bus. Once I got done dropping them off at home I had to turn right back around and start picking them back up for school.

By the time I finished my bus route the next morning the story had reached Hills coffee shop downtown and there was a woman on the school board who was for running my ass out of town right then and there. An emergency school board meeting was held that night and they were all over me. This was serious and I figured my goose was cooked. I kept thinking about how a guy with no degree, who was fired from his first coaching job for keeping teenage girls out until 3:00 A.M. and acting crazy was ever going to get another job. And exactly how I was going to explain this to Mary. I make her move to the middle of nowhere and I promptly get fired? I was all covered up with trouble until my players, every one of the boys and the girls, showed up and supported me. They said they liked me. So I got to keep my job. They saved me. Those tough kids from Benjamin saved me. My coaching career damn near ended that very first year.

The boys' team went 29 and 10 and near the end of the season we played in a tournament over in Hedley, Texas, a town of about five hundred, about 120 miles to the northwest. I didn't know it at the time, but Hedley was looking for a new coach and the entire school board came to watch me. I guess they hadn't heard about the 3:00 A.M. incident. We won the tournament and immediately afterwards they offered me the job of coaching the Hedley boys' and girls' basketball teams the next season. I appreciated what the people and kids of Benjamin had done for me, but I hadn't come to Benjamin to stick around forever so I couldn't say no. I was making a big jump, from a town of two hundred thirty to a town of five hundred. The problem was the basketball teams were pretty bad and we had a lot of issues to overcome. There were a lot of cotton farms around Hedley, which meant that right after school let out all the kids had to go home and pick cotton. We couldn't practice until nighttime and by then all these kids were exhausted from a day of school and farmwork (not that I cared for that excuse). I rode those kids harder than ever. I was unmerciful, especially on the girls. And it worked. That first year the boys' team went 28 and 5 and the people in Hedley were about ready to build a statue for me. In our district we were immediately the team to beat.

My pride and joy of the Hedley teams was a player named Bobby Roland. He epitomized what I loved about those west Texas farm kids. When he was in eighth grade he couldn't walk and chew gum at the same time, he couldn't play dead, but he listened well and was a hard worker. It took months to teach him how to jump off his left foot and shoot with his right hand, but once he got the hang of it, he was unstoppable. He later went on to play at West Texas State and eventually Texas Western, a testament to what a player can become if he is humble and works hard.

Coaching is important, but a lot of times I thought coaches got too much credit. It is the players who make the plays, and any coach will tell you that if you don't have players you don't win games. Coaching in west Texas high schools was no different.

I remember my players talking once about this boy over in Borger, who used to live in Hedley, and they thought he could really play. His name was Bobby Lesley and I went over one night to watch him play: There was no question he was talented. He was a country kid, I'll tell you that, he looked like he had come straight off the farm to play in the game, with dirt still on him. He was also a good student and extremely cocky from beating up on all those farm kids. I went and talked to his mother and asked if they would consider moving back to Hedley, which was about eighty miles to the south. They said that Bobby could move back but under Texas rules we needed to find him a legal guardian.

Well, I found him one in a hurry, me. I became the guardian and Bobby moved in with a local family, Sue and O'Neill Weatherly. Bobby was just what we needed, some natural talent to go with all of our hard work. His senior year he led us all the way to the state semifinals down in Austin, the farthest Hedley had ever been. I am not sure I can convey how big of a deal that playoff run was for a town of five hundred. It generated so much pride in town, it was all anyone talked about. When you are in a community that small you get excited when anyone pays attention to you, when people realize that you exist. We were such a great underdog story the papers made a big deal of us. We got written up all the time in the *Amarillo Globe-News*, which to us was bigger than *The New York Times* and *The Washington Post* combined. One of the sportswriters who took a liking to us was Eddie Mullens, who would later become the sports information director at Texas Western (upon my recommendation) and is a dear friend to this day.

During that run to the state semifinals I ran into George McCarty, the head coach from Texas Western, again. He came to watch our game in the regionals. Afterward he told me he was going to give up coaching at Texas Western to be its athletic director and was going to recommend that they hire me as head coach. I couldn't believe it. Here I was, just a no-name twenty-seven-year-old coach of a Class B school in a town no one had ever heard of and he wanted to give me a Division I college job? The people at Texas Western couldn't believe it either apparently, because they hired a man named Harold Davis, who had more experience, instead. But George called me after Davis got the job and promised he was going to get me to El Paso eventually.

It was OK, because this was just my third year in Hedley and I was enjoying myself. Once I even set what I believe to be the all-time in the state of Texas (heck, maybe the world) record for most technical fouls in a game. It was in a girls' game too. The game started and right off the bat the ref made this horrible call. I went nuts. Coaches didn't question many calls then in girls' games because no one really cared about women's sports. But I did. I went out on the court screaming and hollering and this ref, he was a real character, he said, "Haskins, you get a technical for every step it takes to get back to that bench." I figured he was joking but I turn around and start walking back and I heard him say, "Twelve, thirteen, fourteen." I wound up with sixteen technicals. They didn't throw you out of games like they do now, which is why I figure I might have the record.

That put us in a pretty good hole. The opposing team sent this ole girl up to shoot the sixteen free throws and she made fourteen of them. It was in the first two minutes of the game and we were down 14 to 2. In girls' basketball that might as well have been a thirty-five point lead. But my girls were either excited that I cared so much or (most likely) petrified of this madman of a coach. We came storming back and wound up forcing overtime. But then all of a sudden my best girl, Jeanie Sanders, fainted right on the court. We got her up but she was out of the game. We finally won the son of a bitch in a great comeback, but I was so mad about Jeanie Sanders fainting, I started throwing things around. I got home and an ole boy who was an agriculture teacher and his wife stopped by. I was all upset and said, "That damn Jeanie Sanders needs to get in shape." And I'll never forget the wife said, "Don, she isn't out of shape, it was just that time of month. Women get exhausted easily then." That time of month? I had never even thought of it. It never entered my mind that girls have times of the month. I didn't even think of them as girls, just players.

A funny thing happened though. After being reminded that girls have different times of the month I guess I lightened up a little bit. I started going easy on the girls, you know, maybe just one sprint when I used to give them ten. At least until one day when two of them came to me and complained that I was favoring the boys more than the girls because I was harder on the boys than the girls. I was shocked. Then two mothers came and said they wanted me to treat the girls the same as the boys, that the girls deserved the same demands as the boys. Well, if they were going to ask for it . . . So I went back to going crazy on them. Boy, I ran their asses for miles that day in practice. The whole event reminded me of a simple lesson: players are players, doesn't matter if it is a girl or a boy, a great player thrives on being pushed hard.

My focus on girls' basketball baffled a lot of people, many of whom didn't think girls should be doing anything more athletic than fixin' breakfast. You couldn't even imagine a Sheryl Swoopes or a Mia Hamm existing. I'd be around town and people used to ask me why, if no one else cares about girls' basketball, why the hell did I. And I would look at them and ask, "Well, do you like to get your ass kicked by losing games?"

It was during my days in Hedley that I started working on finishing my degree. I enrolled in some classes at West Texas State in Amarillo and I would make the one-hundred-fifty-mile roundtrip drive. That's a lot of time to be driving through that flat countryside cursing myself for not taking academics seriously when I was at A&M. It took three years but I got it done, although it really cut into whatever time I would have had for my family. It seemed like every free moment I had was spent getting that degree.

My four years in Hedley (1956-60) were wonderful. My

boys' teams averaged a 29 and 6 record so the town people were really excited about us. Well, almost everyone. I used to stop by the Owl Café downtown sometimes. All the old farmers and ranchers used to hang out down there and you know, there ain't nothin' worse than a bunch of damn farmers and cowboys. They needle your ass. They don't have nothin' else to do. You win a game by five and they ask why you didn't win by ten. That first year, in '56, we were off to a good start and I was feeling good about myself when one morning this old man who had some whiskers was settin' there drinkin' a cup of coffee. He said, "Hey, kid, you are the new coach here, huh?" I said, "Yes sir." And he kinda looked me up and down and said, "Are you gonna do for us what ole Catfish did for Kerry down the road over there?" And I said, "Kerry? Catfish? Hell, I don't know."

I decided to do some research. It turns out Catfish Smith was a basketball coach in the 1930s up at Kerry, about forty miles away. It is a real tiny town, smaller even than Hedley. The school had just ten boys total and back then the state basketball tournament didn't distinguish between school sizes. There was just one division. It was just like *Hoosiers* except in Texas instead of Indiana. The ten boys in Kerry had to compete with giant schools from Houston, Dallas, and Austin. One year Catfish led that team to the state title, beating a team from Ft. Worth in the finals. Needless to say, Catfish was a legend. All anyone said was Catfish "carried them boys to the state title." Not coached, "carried." And here I thought I was doing so well going 29 and 6. But no matter how well we did, someone was going to ask about Catfish. And I knew I wasn't going to do what Catfish did, beating five thousand-student schools from the big cities. What his team did might be the greatest Cinderella story in basketball history.

After four years in Hedley, I was ready for something bigger, I needed a new challenge. Now that I had my degree I was able to get a job in 1960 in Dumas, Texas, a city of about eight thousand a little north of Amarillo. This was a big move for me and the family, which now included four sons. That first year we won the bi-district and we had a team with some real talent. Three of my players went on to play college ball, including Kelly Baker, who was six foot six and became a good player at the University of Texas. We went 25 and 7 that year. The people of Dumas were so pleased that they gave me a brand-new station wagon as a gift and to keep other high schools from poaching me away. I appreciated it, but I wasn't planning on going anywhere. I really thought that we had the talent to win a state title the next year.

And, in fact, Dumas High did win the 1962 state title. But I didn't stay to coach them. In August, before the season, George McCarty was on the phone; after just two seasons at Texas Western Harold Davis had resigned to enter private business. George told me to get to El Paso for an interview. The big time was calling.

FIVE

SHOOTIN' POOL

"I don't like these stories much," Haskins kept saying when I'd prod him about his days of making a living shooting pool.

There were two reasons. One, he wasn't proud of his past as a gambler. He didn't want to glorify it. But it happened and it tells you about the man. Anyone can gamble, but as one of his friends said, "There is gambling and there is accumulating. A pro doesn't gamble."

The other reason Haskins hates these stories is because he feels that simply restating or retelling the facts reeks of bravado. There is no way around it. And Haskins would rather be known as a bad coach than a braggart. So we get this.

"I heard you beat Willie Mosconi once," I said to him.

"Where the hell d' you hear that?" he said.

"Earl Estep," I said, mentioning a college buddy Haskins used to run with who would most certainly know.

"Uh-oh." He paused. "You've been talking to Earl, huh?"

Generally speaking, autobiographies are not supposed to require a lot of investigative reporting. But I don't know who to believe. Did Haskins play Willie Mosconi, one of the most famous pool sharks in history? According to Haskins, no. "Total fiction. I once played an exhibition against a pro from New York though." But Estep says they most certainly played when Haskins was a college student in Stillwater.

"Don was the best pool or snooker player perhaps of all time and I'm not just saying that," said Estep, who basically put himself through college and dental school by gambling, and is now a dentist in Athens, Texas. "One time Willie Mosconi came by Stillwater to put on an exhibition upstairs at Swim's pool hall. Mosconi was an eight- or ten-time world champion at this point and he was paid by the Brunswick Billiards Company. We were all trying to talk Don into coming up and playing Mosconi. A guy like that was always looking for locals to play for money after he put on an exhibition.

"I backed Don one hundred dollars a game of nine-ball and he broke and ran the table. Then he rebroke and ran the table. He went on to run the table a few times. Mosconi never got to shoot. Don beat him. Finally Mosconi walked over, hung up his cue, and said, 'I can't beat this kid.'"

That's a lot of detail for something that didn't happen.

Now, ninety-nine percent of people would be fairly proud of the

time they whipped Willie Mosconi seventeen times in nine-ball.
Even if they didn't do it, a lot of people would let someone else tell
that fish tale and take the innocent glory. Haskins?

"I never played Willie Mosconi. That story is ridiculous."

Said Estep, "Oh, he's gonna downplay it, but I was sitting
there betting the money. It happened. Besides, he called me two
months ago and said if you called not to talk about this or that with
you. Well, after an hour and a half of telling me what I couldn't
talk about there wasn't anything left to tell. So I'm just telling
everything."

Haskins will admit one thing about Mosconi.

"I did see Willie Mosconi play once and I never thought he was
that good of a player. You know how people get reputations. Like
Amarillo Slim, he was always promoting himself."

But he insists he never played Mosconi. Never. So, officially,
Don Haskins did not beat Willie Mosconi in a game of nine-ball
in Stillwater, Oklahoma. He didn't even want this story in the
book. But why, I asked him, would Earl Estep make up the
story?

"Ole Earl, he lies a little bit," Haskins laughed.

I am not so sure he is the only one.

■

If there was one thing, other than coaching, I was pretty good
at in my life it was shooting pool. The problem is gambling,

hustling, and playing nine-ball and snooker is a sickness and it almost got me in a lot of trouble a number of times.

One of my jobs as a kid was racking balls at Harold's Snooker Parlor in Enid, Oklahoma. It wasn't a real tough job, so I had plenty of time to learn how to hit balls too. At an early age, I learned how to play. By the time I was seventeen, I had run a snooker table. I'd run a nine-ball table, three, four games in a row. You make one and it is over. Just like on television. Snooker was really my game. In nine-ball, a monkey can beat you every once in a while. In snooker, if you are ten percent better than the other guy, you can toy with them. That's why it is a better game to hustle.

When it comes to pool there are hustlers all over this country and there were a couple of them in Enid. They were older guys, about thirty-five, forty who gambled for a living. By the time I was in high school, I was as good as they were, so they decided to have me join them. They hired me to help in some hustling. I was young and this sounded like more fun than lugging sacks of wheat or flipping burgers or whatever jobs guys my age had back then. I told my mother I was going on a fishing trip for a week, but I went with them instead. I was young looking and real skinny, with thick, tough hair that would cause Mr. Iba to nickname me Rope when I was at A&M because it looked like strands of rope.

We took off and went all over. Albuquerque, Cheyenne, and all sorts of little towns in between. It didn't matter where. As long as a town has a pool hall it has a pool champion. There is always a champion. You find the champion and then you beat him. What we did was an old-style hustle. The guys I was with would play, get a feel for the competition, and then run the kid (me) in on them. They'd weed out the champion, lose a few bucks to him, and then claim, "Hell, my little brother can beat you." The champion would fall for it just about every time, the stakes would get raised, side bets would be made with the champion's friends. I'd play, whip the champion, and pretty quickly we'd clean the place out. Gambling has a lot of bullshit in it.

I saw the same scam twenty years ago in El Paso. I was down at the King's X, a pool hall here in town, just knocking some balls around, not for money or anything (I stopped doing that when I got to be a college coach), just playing for fun. In comes this little blond-headed kid, about nineteen. He was with two older guys. And they were playing and lost a game. I knew what was happening, so I watched as one of the older guys said to someone, "Hell, I bet you can't take my little brother" and asked for a couple hundred. I just laughed. That little blond kid, skinny as a rail, he could play.

But these guys weren't after just anybody. They were after the best player in El Paso, a guy named Bobby. I hadn't played in ten years and he could beat me by only a little. So he was good, but he wasn't good enough. Well, pretty soon they bring in Bobby. It was a typical hustle. Nobody is looking for the best in the world, just for the best in that town, because normally he ain't that good. And you know it. But he doesn't. Since he beats everyone in the town, he thinks he just might be the best in the world. And the ego makes him easy to hustle.

I'm telling you, a hustler is a terrible thing. I am serious when I say it is worse than bein' a bank robber. At least the bank robber is honest in what he is doing—he walks in and demands the money. A pool hustler doesn't have that kind of courage. But he is still stealing money. Pool hustling gets glamorized, but it is still about taking people's money. But I didn't realize that for years.

When I was in college I was sick. I felt like anytime I needed a little money I could go hustle a little bit. The problem was, I always needed some money. I was married and had a child. Mary was able to get a secretarial job on campus that paid about $175 a month. I got fifty dollars a month for housing. That was all we had. Oklahoma A&M wasn't one of those programs where a booster was going to give you some extra cash. And there wasn't a man tough enough to dare ask Mr. Iba for a handout. He was rougher than a wood hauler's ass, so you wouldn't think of doing it. So $225 a month was all we had. You think that isn't a hell of a way to raise a family? When you are in that kind of a situation, the baby has to eat, you have to do what you have to do. For me, that meant hustling pool.

When I played at Oklahoma A&M it was before television, so once you got outside Stillwater no one knew who you were. They might know your name from radio or newspapers, but not what you looked like. For about a year in college I would go every Saturday to Drumright, Oklahoma, which was about twenty miles from campus. I had found out about a nine-ball game in Drumright, just two dollars to get in, always about seven or eight guys. We always had basketball practice on Saturday mornings and afterwards I would put on some jeans and a little white T-shirt with some oil on it. The other guys at the bar thought I worked out in the fields for Shell Oil.

A deal like that you can't get greedy. No one in the bar could play so I would never hit a combination in or anything like that. I would make my seventy or eighty dollars and leave. Never more than that. It was never big games, the bar just had a big sign up and it said, "Open Game." Well, one day the jig was up. I walked in, got my stick, and sat down waiting for an opening to play. But everyone in the bar put down their sticks. They had found out I was a snooker player and a basketball player at A&M and not an oil worker. Someone must have told them or recognized me, I don't know. I never found out. I just left after that. It was a wonder I didn't get the hell beat out of me by seven or eight boys.

Shooting pool was obviously becoming a problem for me. I was married and had a son and I was putting myself in some bad situations. One time, my wife almost left me. It was just before I was to leave Oklahoma A&M. I was fixing to go to Artesia to play basketball and decided I needed some money. I played an ole boy from Oklahoma City. His name was Harris and he was about fifty. We played at Swim's, right in Stillwater. We played a game that lasted two nights and three days. We played all day and all night, no breaks other than to go to the bathroom. By the end I just wore him out. He got tired. I won a couple of cars and about twenty-seven hundred dollars. I sold one of the cars and kept the Pontiac for a while. I actually drove it into Benjamin, Texas, for my first job. But anyway, when you are away from your wife and young son for three days and two nights, well, it wasn't a surprise mama wasn't really happy when I came home. We had a little discussion about this and I swore I wouldn't play again. And I did quit for a while.

I had a friend in college named Earl Estep, who would later go on to become a dentist in Athens, Texas, and to this day is still a great friend of mine. Earl is a smart guy who had played basketball at A&M for a year, but he was always gambling and taking the money of the rest of the team. Finally, Mr. Iba called him in and told Earl that he had to stop gambling, he was hurting the other players. Earl told Mr. Iba that maybe he should tell the other players to stop gambling, since it was they who were losing. "It doesn't seem like I've got the problem," Earl reasoned. Mr. Iba smiled a little at that logic, but Earl wasn't that good of a basketball player. He was expendable. So he had to choose between the basketball team and playing cards. Earl chose cards. He could make five times what a scholarship was worth gambling and he wound up getting a dental degree because of poker.

Earl favored poker to pool because he knew how to fix the deal, meaning he could give you just about any hand he wanted you to have. Four queens, a bunch of junk, whatever. That tends to make you a hell of a poker player. He'd deal a guy four sixes and the guy would bet the house and then Earl would turn up with four sevens. He could set it up so a weak player would wipe out a strong player and then Earl would just beat the weak player. He was that good.

Just after I had swore to Mary I was quitting, Earl said to me, "Don, I heard of a guy over in Pond Creek, Oklahoma, who is the world's champion snooker player." Well, he knew how to get me going because I couldn't stand it. Just saying that was telling me there was some easy money to hustle in Pond Creek. Like I said, I was sick in the head. It was only about sixty miles to get there and I had some money stashed away, so one afternoon we went to Pond Creek. Earl takes me to a little beer bar that had a little snooker table.

The problem with Estep was he could get you in trouble with his mouth. Subtlety is not one of his strengths. We got there and start beating these balls around and all these farmers were looking at us in their overalls. Nothing was really happening so Estep got bored and suddenly said to the bar, "This ole blond-headed boy can beat anyone's ass in Pond Creek, Oklahoma." Well, if you want to get a game going quick, just do that. About ten minutes later this ole boy showed up and said, "What do you want to play for?" Normally I don't bet that way with someone because hell, I don't know how good he is, but then again, snooker is not a luck game. I could play well enough to let a guy get close but never win.

We set up a one-game bet. Earl and I are on one side and Pond Creek on the other. The bets just kept getting bigger and bigger. By the end there were fifty people jammed into this little place and Pond Creek probably had only 350 residents. We even got the money out of the cash register, every last cent everyone there had. Four hundred some odd dollars was on the game, which was a lot of money back then. Estep had our money out to match. I told him I didn't want to be there all day, so I got it done. The other guy couldn't play a lick. I could have spotted him thirty-five points and still won. We wound up cleaning out the bar. After I beat him, we had a damn hard time getting into that car. We had every farmer in Pond Creek after us. Estep was about six foot four and I was six foot one, so we could handle ourselves, but we were outnumbered. I just wanted to get back to Stillwater before someone pulled a gun on us. But not Estep. As we are getting into the car he says, "Any of you son of a bitches want to play poker?" They are ready to tattoo our asses and he is trying to get a damned card game going. I tried to shut his ass up. Hell, they used to shoot guys for less out in Oklahoma. So we get out of there, lucky to be in one piece. We had broken the whole town. On the way home I gave Estep hell for getting greedy and reminded him that anytime you clean the cash register out, well, that is what one would call a good day of work, a good day at the office. But hell, you have to leave a man the britches on his bottom, his dignity, or you are gonna wind up on the wrong end of a gun.

When I was playing for the AAU club in Artesia I don't think any of my teammates thought I knew what color the eightball was. We'd be on the road for games and go to a little bar and I would just sit back and watch, maybe read the paper. I was trying to go cold turkey. It lasted until that year in Benjamin. There was nothing to do in that town, no bars, no movie theaters, just one little restaurant. There wasn't anywhere to get a beer, even a store that sold them, within forty, fifty miles. This was fine, because if you were a schoolteacher in Texas in those days you didn't shoot pool and you sure as hell didn't drink. What I did for fun was call coyotes and hunt them. I met a state gaming employee in Benjamin who taught me how to call a coyote by using this whistling device that sounded like a dying rabbit. For some reason, I was a natural at it. To this day I can call a coyote almost anytime I want. Even when we didn't hunt them we'd call the coyotes down from the hills outside of town just for the fun of it. I know that doesn't sound like much in the way of entertainment, but you had to do something in those towns.

I did fall off the wagon though. It was Christmas and I hadn't had a beer in months. Because of basketball practice, I didn't have much time off for Christmas so I drove Mary and Mark to Lawton, Oklahoma, where they got picked up by Mary's mother to spend the holiday with her family. I was driving back to Benjamin and I couldn't wait to drink a beer. Just one. I pulled into Wichita Falls, Texas, and found a place called the Pheasant Lounge. It was just a little bar, ten stools, but it had a snooker table. In walks a guy about forty who was wearing a cowboy hat. I was drinking my beer, not bothering anyone, when he asks if I want to play snooker for a beer. Well, that's no big deal, I figure, the guy wants to be friendly. So I said, "Sure." Then he immediately says, "You want to make that for two dollars and a beer?" I thought, Well, this son of a bitch . . . he is trying to hustle me. We play and I keep letting him come close and then beating him and then letting him double the bet. The whole time I kept thinkin',

Yeah, you finally found someone you couldn't hustle. After a couple hours we'd drawn a pretty good crowd.

I made $2,810 a year in Benjamin. I wasn't hustling pool anymore so things were a bit tight. I needed some money, bad. They had a leather satchel at the bottom to hold the balls and that is where, after each game, he kept stuffing his money in there to cover the bet. I was into his money. I hadn't taken a penny out of my pocket. There was about one hundred dollars in there—that was almost three months of my rent—when I decided enough was enough. I just wanted to get the cash, get out of Wichita Falls, and go back to being a straight arrow coach. So I say, "That's it," and started to reach for the bag. The guy I was playing stepped in front of me and whipped out a deputy sheriff's badge and said, "I think you should just be moving on. I was just kidding." He grabs the money and starts toward the door. I came close to hitting the SOB, but that would have ended my coaching days. The crowd got angry and started giving him hell and I shouted at him all the way to his car, but what are you going to do? I never got my hundred dollars.

That was the end of my gambling days until five years later. In 1961, when I coached in Dumas, Texas, and I took up a new pursuit, golf. They had made me coach of the Dumas High golf team even though I didn't know how to play. But I was out there screwing around with golf every day and I was starting to make progress. There was an ole boy who had a big ranch and was a wheat farmer. He had a lot of money and was a prominent person around town. He would come out and want me to play him in golf. Now, you know my past. He wanted to play for money but that would have been dumb, you don't beat a big-time guy in town for money. So I kept saying no.

It is at this point that George McCarty, the ex-coach of Texas Western, is calling me all the time, telling me he eventually wanted me to replace Harold Davis as head coach in El Paso. I had expected to coach another year of high school until one day in August of 1961 George calls and says, "Hey, Hoss, you have to come down for an interview, but you have the job." So I've got the job at Texas Western and I am going to be leaving town. Why not give the old rancher what he's been beggin' for? It's the least I could have done, right?

So I went out to the course, we got on a cart, and we played one hole. And I screw up on purpose. And he says, "What do you want to play for? Come on, Coach, damn, let's play for something. I can't stand playing for nothing." We start playing one hundred dollars a ball with two balls. All I want to do is knock him off enough to pay for my move out of town. We played all day. And when I say all day, I mean all day. Sunup to sunset and by the end I won about twelve hundred dollars, a ton of money. I just wiped him out. He was so rich he thought it was funny. He kept saying, "Damn, Coach, for months I couldn't get you to play for fifty cents and now you'll play for twelve hundred dollars?"

Yeah, well, that's how hustlers do it.

SIX

TEXAS WESTERN

When he looks back on it now, over four decades later, Nolan Richardson can't help but laugh. Don Haskins may not have had a piece of straw between his teeth when he came to the city, but he might as well have. The guy was pure country and while El Paso isn't exactly New York City, some of Haskins's new players were actually from New York City.

Hurdles arose between the demanding white farm coach and the cool black city kids on that first team. There was the style of play— all defense, no showboating. His fashion sense: "He wore a clip-on tie," said Richardson. "We always used to laugh at that." Then there was his dialect and accent—a deep Okie drawl full of colorful country sayings.

To call it a culture clash doesn't do that first year justice.

"He was a typical country boy," said Richardson, a 1963 graduate of Texas Western. "We couldn't understand the things he was saying. We had four blacks on the team that first year and we didn't understand a word of it."

Take the afternoon Haskins came out and accused a white player, Bobby Lesley, of "barbershoppin'," which, to Haskins, meant gossiping because that is what people do at the barbershop. "In a small town, you go down to the barbershop and within fifteen minutes you've heard all the town's gossip," Haskins said. This was a term lost on the city guys.

"Willie Brown comes over to me and says, 'Did Bobby ask Coach if he could go to the barbershop?' " said Richardson. "Bobby's got some kind of huevos nerve asking Coach stuff like that."

Eventually Richardson and Brown asked the country guys to translate and a funny thing happened. The phrases and the lessons surrounding them stuck. Richardson went on to become a successful college coach himself, the only one ever to win an NCAA, NIT, and national junior college championship.

And even into the 2001 season at Arkansas he found himself repeating those old sayings to an even more modern group of teenagers.

"There was something going on and I said to my team, 'I don't need any barbershoppin' here,' " Richardson laughed. "And I stopped and just thought, Damn . . . did I say that?"

∎

When it came to job interviews I wasn't the most experienced guy in the world, but even I knew that the one that I had for the Texas Western Miners head-coaching position was a bit unusual. In August of 1961, at age thirty-one, I drove down to El Paso to meet Dr. Ray, the Texas Western president, my old friend George McCarty, now dean of men, and Ben Collins, the football coach and new athletic director, who is one of the finest people I have ever known anywhere in my entire life.

The interview didn't take long. We were all standing there quietly when Dr. Ray mentioned they were having some problems with rowdy football players in the athletic dormitory. Then he said, "You're a big guy, can you take care of that damn dorm?" I had no idea what this had to do with coaching basketball, but I said, "Yes sir." That was the correct answer and he offered me the job. He never asked me if I could coach. He never asked me about my vision for the program, how I would recruit, schedule, or sell tickets. He never asked me about playing for Mr. Iba, or why he should hire a high school coach from the tumbleweed panhandle of Texas. He and Ben simply took George's word for it. George was the one who knew basketball and he had vouched for me, telling them I was a good coach and once I said I could get that damn dorm under control, I was hired. This also might tell you about the state of college basketball, how seriously (or not seriously) it was taken, especially in west Texas. Here was another sign: I took a significant pay cut to come to TWC. I was making nine thousand dollars a year coaching high school basketball in Dumas and had just received a new station wagon from the boosters. TWC was paying only sixty-five hundred dollars. College basketball just wasn't popular in Texas. To make it I would have to move my family into the athletic dorm where we could live and eat for free at the school cafeteria. Mary was behind it though, and I wanted to be a college coach. With the opening of the new, forty-six-hundred-seat Memorial Gym, I thought we could win. I never hesitated with the decision.

The first player I ever met at Texas Western was Nolan Richardson. He was a sophomore and was sitting on the front steps of the athletic dorm waiting for me when I pulled up in a U-Haul truck full of family and furniture. He shook my hand and helped us move in. Nolan had been a three-sport star athlete (basketball, football, and baseball) at Bowie High in El Paso and was a promising young player for Texas Western. He would go on to be a successful college coach himself, winning the 1994 NCAA title at Arkansas. He's a legend in El Paso, the town even named a middle school after him. He's a quality guy and someone whom I have stayed very close to throughout my life. He has been a great friend and someone I could always count on.

I don't think Nolan liked me much that first week though. I arrived in El Paso on August 3 and I immediately asked Ben Collins when we could start practicing; I couldn't wait to get started. You know, when you're young, you're en-thusiastic, and I just wanted to get going. Ben said he didn't know when I could start. I think he was surprised, that I wanted to start practice so early. The football team had barely started their two-a-days. I said, "Can I start tomorrow?" And he said, "Sure." It turns out we weren't supposed to start prac-ticing until October, but I wasn't aware of that rule. So the day after Nolan helped us unload that U-Haul, we got after it. Now, talk about some brutal workouts. I knew only one way to coach college kids and that was Mr. Iba's way. Three-a-days. No water. Sometimes no breaks. I look back on it now and I realize I was unmerciful. I was wrong. I'd practice them all night if I felt like it. We went over everything. The reason for all of this was because of our schedule. I saw the first three games were against tremendous competition—at Iowa State, Tulsa, and Oklahoma A&M. These were three big-time teams, all of them ranked in the top twenty. I didn't want these teams to crush us, especially Oklahoma A&M. I think I was petrified to return to Stillwater with a terrible team and have Mr. Iba embarrass me.

So I worked them, and worked them, and worked them. I was freed from the restrictions of high school, where parents would wonder where their kids were, and I was making the most of it. It's funny, but Nolan thought I was out of my mind and he, like most of my players, probably hated me at the time. The same way I hated Mr. Iba. The thing we worked on most, just like Mr. Iba, was half-court man-to-man de-fense. To me, you have to guard someone if you expect to win. And in 1993-94, the year Nolan won the national title, he had all these athletes running a full-court pressure defense they called "forty minutes of hell." He had a great team. I told him at the beginning of that year in 1993, "Nolan, you'll win a lot of 'em with that defense, but when it comes right down to the last two or three games, the Final Four, if you don't have a good half-court defense, you won't win." And he won that year with a good half-court defense. That was Mr. Iba's defense.

I think athletic director Ben Collins's faith in me was shaken a bit, however, when my first recruit showed up. It was Bobby Lesley, who I had once "adopted" when I coached in Hedley. The first week I got to El Paso, Bobby called me. After Hedley, he had gone to Clarendon Junior College in the Texas panhandle and was a star. Schools from all over the country wanted to sign him and he had agreed to go to Rice. They had even set him up with a high-paying job in the west Texas oil fields outside Odessa and Midland for the summer. The job was big money and it was designed to keep him loyal to them. However, this was before the binding national letter of intent, so because of the job, when other schools tried to come in and poach him, he was expected to tell them he was going to Rice. He heard I got the head job at TWC and out of the blue he called me. He hardly even asked me if I wanted him, he just said, "I think I'll come out to Texas Western, whaddya think?" And I said, "That sounds OK."

I knew how talented Bobby was and I wanted him as a player. But he had gotten married, so I asked him, "Don't you think you should go to Rice?" I didn't have the resources or connections to get him any job at all, let alone one with a comparable paycheck. He said, "No, they just got me that job for the summer, I don't owe them anything." So the very next day he packed up, went out and worked a full day in the oil fields, and quit. He drove to El Paso, pulled up in front of the athletic dorm, and parked his car. He got out barefoot, burr-headed, wearing no shirt, and covered with dirt and oil. He looked like a redneck oil field worker, not a college basketball player.

I had an office that overlooked the parking lot and Ben Collins the AD was in there with me when Bobby pulled up. Ben took one look at Bobby, got out of the car, and said, "Who the hell is that?" And I said, "Hey, that's Bobby Lesley, he is one of my players from Hedley. He's my first recruit." Ben went over and closed my office door and said, "Now Don, I don't know if you know anything about the Border Conference, but we've got Arizona and Arizona State in this league. You are going to have a hell of a time winning with these boys coming in barefooted from Hedley." I just laughed. As it turned out, Bobby Lesley was Ben's favorite player. Ben came to me later that season and said, "The next time you find one of those ole boys from Hedley, you just bring him in." Could Bobby shoot from fifteen, seventeen feet? I never had one who could stick it like he could. He'd have the ball right in front of you and then he'd drive right by you. Bobby Lesley could just play. After he graduated from Texas Western, he became a heck of a high school coach in El Paso and went on to win some five hundred games and a state championship at Eastwood High School. He is in the El Paso Sports Hall of Fame for his coaching career.

That same month I also signed a black kid named Willie Brown from New York, who would become a great player, a big success in business, and later instrumental in helping me to recruit the core of my 1966 national championship team. Harold Davis, the previous coach, had started recruiting him before he left, but Willie had never signed an official scholarship. When I got the job I started receiving a letter from Willie every day asking me to give him a scholarship, which is generally the opposite way that recruiting works. Every day here came a letter. Willie was desperate to get out of New York. I figured that if a guy is writing me every day it must mean he couldn't play dead. If he were any good he wouldn't have to plead his case. My wife, Mary, however, got wind of all of these letters and she liked him for his hunger. She was impressed with him. It was rare for Mary to get involved in recruiting but on this occasion she encouraged me to sign Willie.

I'm glad she convinced me, although I wasn't at first. When Willie arrived that August I met him at El Paso International Airport and he had a big mustache. My first words to him, even before "Hello" were "Shave that damn thing off." I thought I had made a mistake. I certainly didn't need any cool fellas from New York with mustaches on my team. But it turned out to be no mistake. The next day he showed up to practice slick, clean shaven. And then during practice he played so well that I wrapped an arm around his shoulder and told him, "Willie, you can grow a little bit of it back." He didn't dare. I think he thought I was joking.

We'd have had more players in the beginning but that first month of practice was so ridiculous that four guys quit before school started. A couple of them just disappeared into thin air, never heard from them again. Losing players doesn't usually help your team but those kinds of guys, the kind that don't want to practice hard, they are exactly the kind of guys that'll get your ass fired. You are better off in the long run without them.

Right off the bat I worked on getting the guys better. I took Nolan over to the free-throw line. Although all he had done the year before was shoot, he couldn't shoot well and his form was off. He had averaged over twenty points a game, but he had his elbow way out of line. He needed to work on his form. Of course, he didn't think anything was wrong with his form and he, naturally, tested me. He pitched me the ball and said, "Could you show me how?" Show him? Hell, my pleasure. Without warming up I made about seventy-five in a row, because I had learned to shoot on that carnival rim. Then I told him I was gettin' a little tired. And he never said another damn word about shooting form. He started paying attention.

A couple weeks into preseason camp with my roster dwindling, I got tipped off to the first Bobby Joe Hill. I call him the first because he was not the Bobby Joe Hill who would play on the 1966 national championship team. Same name, different player. The 1966 Bobby Joe was from Detroit.

The first one was from Texas, and the only reason I got him was because no one else could take him. Bob Rogers was a guy who played at Oklahoma A&M four or five years before I did. He was now the coach of Texas A&M. I hadn't been at Texas Western two weeks when he called and said, "There's a black kid down here that I can't take." At the time Texas A&M was still segregated. But obviously we weren't. So I am interested and I asked Bob where he played in high school. Bob said, well, it wasn't quite like that. He spent time in a reformatory in Huntsville, Texas. A reformatory? Why the hell would I want a guy out of a reformatory?

But Bobby Joe was from Bryant, Texas, which is the town right next to College Station, just a couple miles from the A&M campus. Bob knew him and promised me he wasn't a bad kid. "I'd take him in a second if I could take a black guy," he said. I knew Bob wouldn't steer me wrong, but I decided to check with the sheriff over in Bryant anyway. I got him on the phone and he said, "Oh, yeah, I remember that Hill boy." It turns out Bobby Joe and two of his friends broke into a Laundromat and, this part I will never forget, they stole $3.75. That's it. I am not saying it is right to steal $3.75—you can't be a little bit pregnant when it comes to stealing—but I'm not sure a buck and a quarter haul each merited arresting all three of them. Do you think that would have happened if they were white? The sheriff, to his credit, said that day, "I'm goin' to tell you the truth, if them boys weren't colored they wouldn't have been arrested." That was just one of the many things blacks dealt with back then. Do something stupid and all of a sudden you are behind bars. There was no room for error. All three pled guilty and the judge offered them a choice, enlist in the Army or Navy or go to the youth reformatory (basically, a low-security jail). The other two enlisted, but Bobby Joe said he'd rather go to jail. He spent six months in there working in the library and getting his GED. When he got out he enrolled at Wharton Junior College in the Houston area. So I called the coach at Wharton and he said, "He's a good kid, but he is lazy. He can play though." That coach was correct on both accounts.

The first Bobby Joe Hill could really play. He was six foot four and was a great defender and rebounder. At this point, about half my team had quit and were probably on outbound Greyhounds never to be heard from again, so I needed some warm bodies. I told Ben Collins all about Bobby Joe Hill and he said, "I don't know." I don't blame him. From his point of view this new coach he hired has brought one recruit in barefoot from an oil patch, has current players quitting because they are practicing from sunup to sundown, and now he wants to sign a forward who was in jail. We decided to take it to the school president, Dr. Ray. He said, "I don't see anything wrong with that. You checked him out." So in came the first Bobby Joe Hill. Now all of a sudden, I have got myself some guys. We were one small team, but we could play defense. I had Bobby Joe, Willie Brown, who at five foot eleven they called Little Oscar after Oscar Robertson, Bobby Lesley, and Nolan, who was getting his shot straightened out and learning a little about playing defense. I had some good players that first year.

One interesting thing was the racial makeup of my team.

I had been around some great teams and great players at Oklahoma A&M. We were always ranked in the top five, but we were all white. It wasn't until I was a junior in college that I even played against a black person. And since I had coached only in small Texas high schools, I had never coached a black player before. Not since Herman Carr had I even really been around a black guy. But Texas Western is a school that integrated in 1955. By 1956, two blacks, Cecil and Charlie Brown, were on the basketball team. By the standards of the day, not much was made of it, probably because El Paso, by sitting on the Mexican border, is such a racially integrated place. These days the city is over eighty percent Hispanic and no school in the country graduates more Hispanic engineers than UTEP. By the time I was named coach, having a black player on the team was nothin'.

Everyone has always asked me what it was like coaching black players for the first time. But for whatever reason, I never even thought about it. Really, I didn't. When I looked out on the floor I didn't see white guys and black guys, I saw players. There was no difference. I treated every one of them the same. All I was interested in was *stoppin'* somebody from gettin' the ball in the basket and then at the other end of the court *gettin'* the ball in the basket. That's it, that's all. If you were doing that, I was happy with you. If you weren't, you were going to hear about it. I don't think it was very different from coaching boys and girls in high school. Other people may have seen a difference, I just wanted to win the game. You can ask any of my players, I treated my white guys and my black guys exactly the same. I don't think it was because I was some enlightened individual, it wasn't a conscious thing. I think it was that I was obsessed with basketball and I didn't want to go into that opener against Iowa State and get my ass beat.

Once I got some players I think I turned up the intensity of practice, if that was even possible. I saw we had a shot to do something that season. It was late August and we would start practicing in the morning even before the football team. We wouldn't be done until after they finished. That's a tough day, man. You have to consider the situation too. Anyone who has ever been in El Paso in August can tell you that hot doesn't even begin to describe the temperature. This is the high desert, right on the Mexican border. It is a dry heat, but every day is around one hundred degrees. In 1961 there was no such thing as an air-conditioned gymnasium.

I knew my guys hated me. The old guys couldn't believe how bad things had gotten since I arrived. The new players were wondering what they were thinking coming here and were probably trying to find out if their bus ticket to El Paso was round-trip. One day we worked until about 9:30 P.M. and I'd really been on their asses. After practice I was sittin' outside the gym smoking a cigarette and trying to get cool. Just above where I was standing was an open window into the locker room. Bobby Joe Hill, Nolan, and Willie Brown, who by then I was calling Willie Catfish, were red-assing up a storm and I could hear every word. Willie was calling me a mother-this and mother-that and Nolan was calling me a honky and that really pissed me off because at the time I didn't even know what that meant. And on and on it went. That got me going. Man, was I getting angry. I couldn't wait to get a hold of them the next day. At the start of practice I lined them up and told them I could read minds and I knew what each one had been saying about me. They looked at me like I was crazy, but then I repeated each thing they said, word for word. They just stood there dumbstruck, wondering how the hell I knew, and more importantly, what I was going to do. They didn't have to wait long because I rode their asses like a borrowed mule. About four years later Willie Brown came back to El Paso after a stint in Vietnam and he asked me how the hell I knew what they had said. He still hadn't figured it out.

A couple days after that I was on my way back to the athletic dorm and there were a bunch of cops there. They had Bobby Joe Hill in handcuffs and were hauling him away to jail. I couldn't believe it. It turns out he hadn't told his parole officer he was going to college in El Paso, so when he failed to show up for a meeting they put out an arrest warrant. I tell you, the dumb things a college coach has to deal with. All he had to do was tell his parole officer what was up and shift his parole meetings to El Paso. I mean, what parole officer wouldn't be thrilled that a guy had gotten a college scholarship? But Bobby Joe hadn't bothered to do that. I hadn't been there three weeks and already my list of incidents was growing. I went over and I told Dr. Ray. He picked up the phone and called somebody down at the jail to get things worked out. For all I knew I was about to get fired. I had staked my word on this kid and it took only a week for the cops to show up. No coach in the country wants to be standing in his president's office asking if he can help get a player out of jail. Let alone a brand-new coach who hasn't been on the job three weeks or won a single game.

But instead of firing me or even cautioning me, Dr. Ray looked at me and said, "You know, I feel sorry for that boy. There's a few times I could have been thrown in the pokey and wasn't. I got lucky." Good ole Dr. Ray, the greatest president a coach could ever ask for! I went down to the El Paso jail, bailed Bobby Joe out, and chewed his ass all the way back to the athletic dorm. Then the next day I really let him have it. He practically ran the Boston marathon in wind sprints.

By the start of the season in November, I was feeling good about my team. We didn't have any size, my biggest guy was about six foot five, but they were the workingest sons of bitches I had ever seen. I thought we had a chance to be OK, but I worried about the schedule for the start of the season. We had those three money games, at Iowa State, at Tulsa, and at Oklahoma A&M. Money games are a long-standing tradition in college sports. It is when a bigger, wealthier school pays a smaller school to come and play them. A big school can make the money back in gate receipts. These days basketball teams can get up to forty-five thousand dollars for one game. If Kentucky wants to play UNC-Greensboro, then it pays forty-five thousand dollars for Greensboro to come to Lexington. Kentucky makes the money back in ticket sales and never has to go to Greensboro. The smaller school usually loses because they are playing on the road and in front of the other team's fans. On the college basketball pecking order, Texas Western, then and now, was down the line, meaning we were being paid to come and play. But I wasn't interested in starting the season 0 and 3, no matter how much money we were making.

So in October, we rode a bus up to Ames, Iowa, and on the way stopped in Lubbock to scrimmage Texas Tech. I stopped feeling good about my team because Texas Tech whipped us. They had a good team, but we shouldn't have gotten beat like we did. We didn't play much defense, we didn't play together, and we didn't play with enough effort. The game didn't count in the standings, but it counted to me. After the game I didn't let my guys shower and change. Instead we found a gym and practiced right through the night. It was just like we were in Benjamin except no one's mommy or daddy was coming to rescue them. I rode those guys straight through until five in the morning, a good eight hours of practice *after a game*. It was unmerciful, just unbelievable now that I think back on it. Not only is something like that against NCAA rules nowadays—heck, it may have been then too—but if a coach tried it now he might get fired. But it was a different time and I didn't care. I didn't want to have my team ever play again like it did in the scrimmage with Texas Tech.

When we showed up at Iowa State we were expected to take a loss and collect our money, which at the time was probably only a couple grand. But my guys were so scared of what might happen if we lost, they didn't even think about how good Iowa State was or about its star player Venny Brewer. I don't blame them. If I practiced them until 5:00 A.M. for losing a meaningless scrimmage to Texas Tech, what would I do if we lost a real game? The morning of the game I read a bunch of local newspapers. All of the Iowa sportswriters were giving the Cyclones a hard time for playing this small, no-name school, Texas Western. I made sure I showed these clippings to every player on my team. I was also hoping that the Iowa State players had read the papers. There is nothing better for a coach than to play an overconfident team while simultaneously having your guys believe they are disrespected.

That night in November of 1961, when I walked out to coach my first college game, I was not the least bit nervous about the actual coaching. I never thought twice about whether I could coach or not. I was probably more worried about having to talk to the Iowa media afterwards than coach the game. As for doing the job, I just knew I could do it. It's not that I wasn't worried about losing, but I was confident in myself. I actually felt a lot better when I saw the Iowa State players in the warm-up lines. I could tell they had read the newspapers because they were looking at us with disdain. My guys were so eager to unleash their pent-up aggression on another team, we went out and won 66 to 59. One of the stars of the game was Bobby Lesley, my barefoot oil field worker who didn't look like much of a player. We weren't tall, but we were so well-balanced and my little guys knew how to play big. Nolan and Willie could defend guys six inches taller. It was a huge upset. Iowa State was a top ten program and had won the Big Eight the season before. After the game, the local media was all over the Iowa State coach for losing to this unheard-of small school. My players were just relieved that I allowed them to shower, change, and go to bed.

The rest of the road trip didn't work out quite as well. We lost to Tulsa by ten and then had to face Oklahoma A&M and Mr. Iba. The last thing I wanted to do was play Mr. Iba, but the game was already scheduled so there was no way to avoid it. Mr. Iba to me was larger than life. I respected his leadership, his intelligence, and the way he carried himself. I just couldn't see a single positive that could come out of playing against his team. And I don't think he saw a benefit in playing one of his former players. I wasn't emotional or introspective about it though. By the time we got to Gallagher Hall I wasn't thinking about playing against my old school and my old coach. By that point, I just wanted to win. My competitive juices were flowing and Oklahoma A&M was just another team I wanted to beat.

Even though we played pretty well, they were better than we were and beat us by six points. The worst part was after the game Mr. Iba invited me into his office to talk and have a Coke and some cookies. What was I going to do? Hell, I was still scared of him. I couldn't say no even though the last thing I wanted to do after a loss was sit down with the coach that just beat me. Even if it was Mr. Iba. I don't think he was too comfortable either, but we sat and talked for a little while and he said he thought I was doing a good job and could win with the team I had. That gave me a shot of confidence. The road

trip was a good thing because we got better from the experience and won our next eight games and eleven of our next
twelve. But it didn't seem like fun losing to Oklahoma A&M.

Throughout my entire career I have obsessed over games
once they were over, even the victories. I would replay the
game in my mind, think of all the mistakes that we made, and
agonize over these things. I know it isn't healthy, but a lot of
coaches are the same way. Before and after games, I was so
concerned that we would never win another game. I was very
pessimistic. But once the ball went up, I never thought we
would lose. After some home games I would just get in my
truck and drive out into the desert all by myself and think
about the game for hours and hours. Just drive around real
slow on country roads, puttering around, obsessing about my
team. I wouldn't want to be around anyone, my players, my
family, Mary, my friends, my assistant coaches. No one. When
we won it would last a couple hours, but after a loss I could
stay out all night.

I know it sounds miserable, but that's the life of a coach.
Or at least this coach.

SEVEN

BAD NEWS

*If you want to sign a top recruit these days, it takes endless travel,
scouting, baby-sitting, ass kissing, and everything else that comes
with dealing with the mamas and the posses. There is a chance
you'll even have to pay someone cash under the table. And then,
after everything, if you are lucky, you get to spend months hoping
the NBA doesn't come a-calling for your player.*

*In 1962 Haskins signed his only junior college All-American
(he never had a high school All-American) by beating him in a free-
throw contest.*

He had just finished telling me the story when I told my own.

"I once heard a similar story," I said. "Denny Crum, the longtime coach at Louisville, tried that trick with Larry Bird. Larry had quit Indiana University after one month as a freshman. He was back in his hometown of French Lick, Indiana. This was before Bird would eventually attend Indiana State, and as a senior lead it to the 1979 national championship game.

"Bird, as you know, was shy. He didn't want to be recruited. He didn't want even to talk to a college coach, but he was too good for coaches to just let him sit there. So Crum drove up from Louisville and found him at his house. Out of respect, Bird came outside, but he didn't have much to say.

"Crum decided to challenge Bird to a game of H-O-R-S-E. If Crum won, Bird would agree to take a visit to the U of L campus. If Bird won, Crum would go away and leave him alone. In the meantime, Crum figured he'd get some time to talk up his program, make a connection, and get the recruiting process started no matter who won the contest. But Bird didn't want to listen. He didn't even say a word.

"Crum got the first shot and missed. Bird then drained five impossibly long, just killer shots that Crum had no chance of making. The game was over within a minute. Larry, without saying a word, promptly shook Crum's hand and went back inside the house. Crum, stunned, his plan backfired, went home with nothing."

Haskins respected Crum, but was dumbfounded.

"Now why in the hell would someone get into a shooting contest with Larry Bird?"

■

Jim "Bad News" Barnes.

In the history of Texas Western/UTEP Miner basketball there may never have been a more important player than Jim "Bad News" Barnes. I'm not saying he was the best, although he may have been. This six-foot-eight man-child who came out of Tuckerman, Arkansas, was not only a great player, but he set the stage for our success in the years to come. My first year as a head coach, the 1961–62 season, we finished with an 18 and 6 record. As I look back on it, that was pretty good; especially since we were young, small, and started the year 1 and 2. At the time, of course, I couldn't believe we didn't win the national championship, or at least the Border Conference. But we got a victory that didn't show up in the win-loss column (at least not that year). That was the year I recruited Bad News.

Barnes was a fantastic player. If they rated high school players then the way they do now, he would have been one of the top five in the country and probably would have gone right to the NBA lottery. He grew up in little Tuckerman, an out-of-the-way town between Jonesboro and Little Rock. If you have ever been between Jonesboro and Little Rock, you know there isn't much there. Regardless, by the time he was a sophomore in high school everyone in four states knew about him. That included Red Loper, the coach of Stillwater High School. Red was ahead of his time. He wasn't content just coaching the kids from Stillwater and waiting around for a good player to come up through the city ranks. He recruited guys to Stillwater High like it was a college. Heck, he recruited better than most colleges, including, at times, better players than Mr. Iba across town at Oklahoma A&M. In 1959, Red had recruited three or four pretty good white guys from around the region when all of a sudden Barnes's mother just happens to move into a house in Stillwater. Red said it was just a coincidence. I was just a high school coach over at Hedley at the time, but since I had ties to A&M I kept hearin' about this Jim Barnes from Stillwater.

Red Loper not only got the players, but took Stillwater barnstorming around the country playing other high school teams. Stillwater was like a high school version of the Globetrotters. He played in four or five different states that year. Big high school teams do that these days, but it was unheard of for a high school in the late 1950s. One day during Barnes's junior season, Stillwater is scheduled to play Pampa High, the Texas state champions. When I heard about the game coming up, I thought, Jim Barnes or no Jim Barnes, Stillwater is going to lose. Pampa is a powerhouse team and Texas has better teams than Oklahoma. Barnes outscored Pampa all by himself and the final score was something like 90 to 50, he just beat their asses. It was an embarrassment to Pampa to get beat so damn bad. It was such a big deal that it made the Amarillo paper. Stillwater went on to beat every team by thirty or forty points. They just dominated that year.

When the district tournament came around, the Oklahoma Interscholastic League decided to investigate just how Jim Barnes moved from Tuckerman, Arkansas, to Stillwater,

Oklahoma. So many other high school coaches had complained about Red Loper's illegal recruiting that they had to do something. It was obvious the deal was sketchy, you can't give an amateur athlete a house and have him maintain his eligibility. So the OIL made Jim Barnes ineligible for one year for being recruited illegally to Stillwater High School. Barnes didn't get to play in the state tournament his junior year.

Stillwater won the state championship anyway; ole Red got the last laugh. He had three or four Division I–caliber players besides Barnes that he had recruited to Stillwater. Since they were white, no one complained. Everyone kept focusing on Jim Barnes. However, the next year the white guys had graduated and Red didn't recruit any new talent because of the uproar over Barnes. All Red had was regular Stillwater kids. The team went something like 3 and 20 in the regular season.

But it turned out Red realized that Barnes's suspension called for him to be ineligible for only one calendar year, like March 1 to February 28, not for one season or even for the rest of his career. So Red brought this to the attention of the Oklahoma Interscholastic League and as a senior Barnes became eligible on the eve of the state tournament, exactly one calendar year after being suspended. Back then everyone got into the tournament no matter the record, so despite its bad record, Stillwater now had a chance because it now had Jim Barnes. He was so good that out of nowhere they streaked to the state championship. So Red Loper won the 1959 and 1960 Oklahoma state titles, with and without Barnes.

Barnes didn't have great grades and since he was black

that meant there were no four-year options for him. Mr. Iba couldn't take him at A&M there in Stillwater because the basketball team wasn't integrated. Barnes went to Cameron Junior College in Lawton, Oklahoma, instead. But I kept my eye on him. His sophomore year at Cameron was my first at Texas Western. A lot of schools were after him at this point, but I had some advantages. First, Moe Iba was Mr. Iba's son and my first assistant at Texas Western. Moe had grown up in Stillwater and went to Stillwater High and was close to Red Loper, who was still in contact with Jim. This, and the coach at Cameron was Gerald Stockton, who had been a teammate of mine at A&M.

Due to getting suspended for one season in high school, Barnes was nervous about taking any payouts or gifts that might have been considered illegal. Stockton talked to him like a father and told him to be very careful. This was good for us because other schools were offering all sorts of extra benefits under the table so if Barnes was looking for money, we would never have gotten him. My entire recruiting budget then was $5,000 and I was living in the dorms with a wife and kids, so even if I had wanted to I had nothing to give Barnes. Everyone was after him, Indiana, Kansas State, Iowa, Utah. He was driving an old car that was held together, no joke, by baling wire. And he later showed me a couple of letters he had received from coaches. One offered a new Impala for signing. The other said he'd never have to attend class. Cheating was big back then and coaches would do anything to get a player who could help them win, and realistically, even though

Barnes said he wouldn't accept any payout, there was a good chance someone would eventually come and buy him.

But I was young and fearless. Even with all my connections and the fact that Barnes was going to play it straight, I had no guarantees. I used up my entire recruiting budget getting to and from Lawton so many times. It was about a twelve-hour drive each way. George McCarty saw the receipts one day and came into my office. Remember, this was my first year. He smoked these big cigars and I'll never forget him looking at me through the smoke and growling, "Hoss, you're blowin' your whole budget on one guy that you probably won't get." Damn I was nervous, Barnes was the only guy I was recruiting at the time. If I missed on him, I was in trouble. I made one last trip up to Lawton that spring. I was completely out of my recruiting money. I think I rolled in on gasoline fumes and knew this would be it. I needed this guy or my program was in trouble. This was the money pool game to end all money pool games. Barnes was hemmin' and hawin' and couldn't make up his mind where he wanted to play college ball. We were talking in the gym and all his teammates were standing around after playing a pickup game. I was out of chances and about at the end of my rope. I couldn't think of anything else to say.

So I bet Barnes that I could beat him in a free-throw shooting contest. He laughed and figured this thirty-something dude would be easy to take, but remember, I could really shoot. He didn't know this. The stakes of the bet were simple. We'd each shoot twenty-five free throws. If he hit more than I did, then I would go back to El Paso and never bother him again. If I hit more, then he would sign with Texas Western right then and there. I told him that to make it fair I wouldn't even take my sports coat off. He laughed, and agreed to the terms of the bet. I knew the odds were in my favor because I had seen him play and knew there was no way he could make more than eighteen or nineteen free throws. I put the scholarship papers down right on the court. He went first and hit seventeen of twenty-five. I got up there and hit the first eighteen with no trouble at all, stopped, and said, "Sign." At this point his teammates were hootin' and hollerin'. He got down on the floor and signed the papers right there, with all of his teammates givin' him hell. It was great. I couldn't believe it, and man, was I relieved.

I don't know if the NCAA had a rule against betting a commitment with a player on a shooting game, but I would have to think it violated some rule or another. So, I guess, I cheated to get Jim Barnes, but it was worth it.

I had told Jim Barnes that he could do for Texas Western what Elgin Baylor had done for Seattle. Before Elgin, Seattle University wasn't much of anything. Elgin turned them into a national power. It was a good motivational pitch, but I also felt it was true. I had been told by Cameron coach Gerald Stockton that my biggest trouble with Barnes would be keeping him motivated, especially in practice. Once he showed up fifteen minutes late for practice and I made him run the bleachers for a couple hours. I was tough on him because he was too good and had too much talent. I couldn't let him slide. I've seen many coaches do the exact opposite and I just can't understand it. They'll let their star slack off and then whip on the bench players. But in my experience I have always found a blue chipper won't quit on you. You owe it to him and your team to get the most out of him. Letting a star cruise is the wrong thing to do.

Barnes was a heck of a talent. He was a natural athlete—strong, quick, and a great leaper. He even had a passion for defense, in part because he could move so well for his size. He could have played about five sports. The only complaint I ever had about Barnes was he was too unselfish. He would pass up shots when he could have easily scored just to keep his teammates happy. Not that he didn't score. As a senior, he averaged 29.2 points a game. In one NCAA tournament game against Texas A&M he had forty-two points. He set so many records at Texas Western, many of which took decades to be broken. Today he still holds more than a dozen school records. Most importantly though, Jim Barnes showed kids around the country that Texas Western was a place where great players played. Nothing attracts great recruits like great players. Barnes was so good that my sports information director, Eddie Mullens, in a promotional effort, hung a nickname on him. He was Bad News Barnes because he was bad news for the opposition.

He made our team better. In 1962–63, during his junior season (but his first with us), we went 19 and 7 and went to the NCAA tournament, the first in the school's history. Mr. Iba brought his Oklahoma A&M team to El Paso to play us that year. It was, thankfully, the last time I had to play Mr. Iba. I wouldn't have done it at all, but it meant a lot to George McCarty to have Oklahoma A&M, a real powerful program, come to El Paso for a game. We had just opened our new stadium, Memorial Gym, so this game was a big to-do. As much as I loved Mr. Iba, I wanted to win this game. And we had a chance. Not only did I have Barnes, but Nolan Richardson was a senior and had really developed. Nolan still couldn't shoot that well, but son of a gun could he guard you. Oklahoma A&M had George Knight, who was the leading scorer in the nation the year before. I stuck Nolan on him and Nolan never let him catch the ball. George got three points in that game. We got up about eight points on the Aggies in the second half and Moe is sitting on the bench moping. I said, "Damn, what's the matter with you?" His dad's sittin' down there getting beat, and while Mr. Iba was my coach and I didn't like it either, I didn't feel as bad as Moe. Moe said, "Well, I wanna beat them by about a point." And I said, "I'll tell you one damn thing. We got beat at your place last year and I had to have a Coke with your dad and talk about the game. I wouldn't mind winnin' by a few more than that."

By the second half, things were still going well for us because of Barnes and Nolan. They were beating up on the Aggies so bad you wouldn't believe it. We just were the better team with the better players. Oklahoma A&M had no answer but Mr. Iba thought he was getting jobbed by the officials and was letting them know about it. He was like Bob Knight, only tougher. At one point he scared the hell out of me. I was watching the game and out of the corner of my eye I saw him charging down the sideline toward our bench. I didn't know whether to go start runnin' wind sprints or what. I was still so scared of him. He was shouting the whole way, "These are the worst officials." I was dumbfounded. I said, "Coach, I didn't get 'em and one of 'em is yours." One of them, the one causing the most problems, was a Big Eight official. We wound up winning that game, but it was one victory I didn't enjoy very much. Beating Mr. Iba was no fun at all, which is why I never played him again. I wouldn't even play Oklahoma A&M even after he retired. I never wanted any part of that ever again because of my personal history with the school.

We finished 25 and 3 Barnes's senior year (1963–64) and darn near won the national championship. In fact, to this day I still think we should have won it. The three games we lost were the games that Barnes fouled out. Barnes wasn't the only great player we had either. We also still had the first Bobby Joe Hill, at least until he flunked out of school in the middle of the 1963–64 season. That didn't help at all. I had tried to get him straightened out academically, but unless you want to write his term papers, you can do only so much. I also had Steve Tredennick, who was a twenty-five-point-a-game scorer from El Paso's Burgess High School, but was a step too slow to be a big-time scorer in college. So he dedicated himself to defense, rebounding, and scoring when needed. I don't know if I ever had a tougher kid or a harder worker. He was just one hard-nosed Texan. I remember trying to break him down, but he wouldn't quit. He didn't know the meaning of the word. It showed in his life also. Steve went on to become a lawyer and has a successful practice in Round Rock, Texas, just outside of Austin.

Our 1963–64 team had a lot of attitude and the one who led the way was Bobby Dibler, a cocky lefthander I had found at Amarillo Junior College. He gave us plenty of swagger. Andy Stoglin was a junior who had transferred to Texas Western. He was tough. Orsten Artis, Harry Flournoy, and Willie Cager, who would all play on the 1966 team, were just sophomores. Artis, in particular, played a lot and became a starter for most games. However, I hardly needed those guys because Barnes was always ready to dominate. We worked so hard at making the ball go through Barnes that guys regularly passed up open shots so he could touch it. We were selfless. We made the top ten of the national wire polls for the first time in the school's history. This was one major deal in El Paso at the time. We were a small, out-of-the-way town, with a little school. No one paid attention to us. So to make the national top ten and have our school's name appear in every newspaper in America, from New York to Los Angeles, was a great source of pride. We started packing the forty-six-hundred-seat Memorial Gym for games. Everyone in El Paso was suddenly a major Miner fanatic. We entered the NCAA tournament with a 24 and 2 record and even though this was just my third season, I thought we had a real shot at winnin' the national championship. As I look back on it, winning a national championship in your third year of college coaching, especially at a place such as Texas Western, would really have been something. But at the time I never thought about it. I never worried about my age (I was thirty-three), my experience, or where we were. I just never even considered it. As far as I was concerned we were in the NCAA and so the goal was to win the NCAA tournament. I was hell bent on getting that done.

We played Texas A&M in the regionals and Barnes scored forty-two points so that was about it for them. A&M had an All-American guard named Benny Lenox, but no one could handle Barnes. If he hadn't been so unselfish and had shot more (he went sixteen of twenty-three from the floor), he could have had seventy points in that game. Anytime he wanted a basket, he had one. For good measure, he also grabbed nineteen rebounds that night. We went up against Kansas State in the next round and the winner would go to the Final Four. This was where the refs killed us. As I said, Barnes had fouled out of the only three games we lost all season. With him we were unstoppable. But without him, we were beatable. Forty years later that game still bothers me because I thought that one referee was fixing the game. I can still see him now. He called five of the quickest, ticky-tackiest fouls you have ever seen on Barnes. K-State played a tight two-three zone on him and Barnes picked up three early fouls just trying to get across the lane. All he was trying to do was move, but he'd bump someone and get the whistle for an off-the-ball offensive foul. I have never in my life seen a player get called for two of those, let alone three. The same referee called all five fouls on Barnes. He wound up playing just eight minutes. Even without him we almost won, but wound up gettin' beat 64 to 60.

The reason I still continue to think that we could have

won the national title that season is because Kansas State went on to the Final Four and lost a close game to UCLA, who later became the champions. This was John Wooden's first championship team at UCLA and they were good, no question. But they had a six-five center and we had Bad News Barnes. There is no way a six-five guy is stopping our guy. Barnes would have dominated. If only that ref had just let him play.

EIGHT

FIVE BLACK PLAYERS

"When was the first time you started five black players?" I asked Haskins.

"Don't remember," he said. "Never thought about it."

"Well, I talked to Nolan Richardson and Andy Stoglin [two players on his 1962–63 team] and they remember. They remember exactly."

"Who?" Haskins laughed.

This was the problem with writing the autobiography of Don Haskins, the anti–self-promoter. Usually, in an autobiography, you have to worry about the subject embellishing positive stories. In

Haskins's case, he just prefers to forget the really good stories altogether. Instead of banging his chest and crying for attention about a decision he made over four decades ago, he tries to change the subject, pretends it didn't matter, or, most often, that it didn't even happen in the first place.

So we have a guy with such an impressive memory he can rattle off the names and favorite brand of beer of four guys he went hunting with in Knox County, Texas, in 1955, but then with a straight face will claim to forget the big stuff.

"This was the thing," said Richardson. "Five black starters were too much for people to handle."

"A lot of coaches," said Andy Stoglin, a 1965 graduate who is black and spent fourteen seasons as the head coach of Jackson State, "would act like racism never existed. A white player would start in front of a black player who was better and the coach would never say anything about it. But everybody knew. Everybody knew."

There is no official record of what game (or even what season) the historic event occurred. Harry Flournoy insists it didn't happen until 1965. Publicist Eddie Mullens, generally the Bible of Texas Western basketball history, can't recall. But one plausible story is that during the 1962–63 season there was a game where Texas Western had five black players good enough to start.

"[Haskins] called me into his office because I was not starting," said Stoglin. "He said to me, 'I know you should start, but I can't start five black players.' He pulled out a drawer from his desk and dumped these letters out and said, 'Read these and tell me what you think.' He left me in the office for thirty minutes. I read some of them. The mail said, 'You're playing too many niggers.' All sorts

*of awful things like that. They said they were going to fire Coach
Haskins.*

*"He came back and told me not to tell the other players about
it. I could tell the pain it was causing him."*

*A couple days later Richardson says he was called into
Haskins's office.*

*"He said, 'Nolan, I need you to do me a favor. I'm probably
not going to start you tonight* [Stoglin was going to start
instead]. *I don't want to get into a situation where I am starting all
black kids. I don't want to deal with what everyone is going to say.
I'm asking you because you're a senior and you're from El Paso
and I think you can handle it.' And I said, 'OK, Coach.' "*

*Richardson and Stoglin said rather than being disappointed in
the decision or getting angry with Haskins, they stood in awe of
their coach for his humbling honesty. There was almost no such thing
as frank talk about race in the early 1960s. White men and black
kids were not equals in most of society. What Haskins was saying,
according to Richardson, took more courage than if he had started all
five blacks. That might have meant he really didn't care, didn't
really know what he was doing.*

*Instead he was acknowledging the situation and admitting a
weakness. The easy thing to do was what every other coach in the
country was doing. Ignore the problem and play a white guy or two.
The players didn't expect anything more than that; instead they got
an honest and rational explanation about the elephant in the room.*

*"That's the kind of man he was, straight up," Richardson said.
"He wasn't making any excuses. He wasn't going to lie. He wasn't
going to ignore it like every other coach in the country. I wasn't mad*

at him, because I was young but I wasn't dumb. I knew exactly where he was coming from."

Then, later, when he started five black players, he proved he was making a courageous decision that went against the norms of the day. That, says Richardson and Stoglin, is the measure of greatness.

"Right before the game that night, he yells, 'Richardson!' And I run over and he says, 'Screw it. You're starting. Screw what they'll say.' And that was it. We started five black players.

"Now," Richardson predicted, "he'll deny that story because he doesn't want to get into it. He doesn't want the controversy. He's too humble. But it happened. Oh, did it happen."

I tell Haskins what Stoglin and Richardson told me.

"I don't remember that," he said. "Andy and Nolan? No, that never happened. No way. I think they are dreaming."

"So," I said, "two different guys, in two different interviews, tell me nearly the exact same story, but I am to believe they are dreaming?"

"I don't remember that," he said.

"You know," I told Haskins, "if you don't start remembering things, this is going to be one hell of an autobiography."

"Did I ever tell you about calling coyotes . . ."

■

I can't remember the exact moment I decided to start five black players although some of the players—namely Nolan Richardson and Andy Stoglin—claim they do. I just have no idea, I don't even know what season for sure, let alone what game. I guess it happened during the 1962–63 season, but only for a game or two. There were times that season when we would play five black players at the same time, which was probably also a first. I know there was one game that year that Bobby Lesley, who was white, didn't play at all because of an injury. So maybe that was it. I don't know. I guess it just worked out one night that the best player we had at each position was black. It wasn't an everyday thing though. At the time most teams in the South didn't have a single black player, but it wasn't uncommon for a school in the North or West to start three or occasionally even four black players. But never, at least according to anyone's knowledge did a team anywhere in the country start five black players.

I don't think I knew it at the time that no one had started five, but I did know it was unusual. I really didn't think about it much. I had enough problems getting these guys—white and black—to play defense the right way.

And I admit that on some level the idea of starting all five of them entered my mind, at least for a second. If I coached in a vacuum, I don't think it would have even dawned on me at all what the race of my players was. Anyone who played for me can tell you I treated everyone the same, that race was not a factor in how I coached the team. But I didn't coach in a vacuum. I coached in crowded basketball arenas where fans would yell things. I coached in an office that received mail from all over the country, nasty, racist, ugly, and angry mail that would come in and call me names. It happened even before I started five of my black players. Naturally there was way, way more of it after we won the national championship, but that was because we became big news. We were on national television and in national magazines and newspapers all over the country. Some idiots out there were upset that we played any blacks. I bet every coach in the country that had black players also received letters. That, unfortunately, was how sick some people were back then; a college kid playing basketball could so anger someone because of his race that they would take the time to write a vicious letter to the coach.

Back then, all the teams from the Atlantic Coast Conference (Duke, North Carolina, Maryland) to the Southeastern Conference (Alabama, Florida, Kentucky) to the Southwest Conference (Texas, Texas A&M, Houston) had only white players. When I played at Oklahoma A&M our teams were all white. I didn't play against a black person until my junior season when we faced Cleo Littleton of Wichita State. These were the times and I lived in them.

So I had read and heard the ugly things. But really, I don't remember fussing or sweating over it. I know Nolan Richardson says otherwise, but all I remember is that I wanted to win and I sure as hell wasn't going to let some letters or fans bother me. Hell, opposing fans will scream at you if you start five white guys. It doesn't matter. Besides, I owed it to my players, my school, and my administration to put the best team on the floor. I certainly wasn't thinking outside of El Paso. I didn't consider how it might affect other schools. I didn't know or care about anything outside of my locker room. If I didn't play my five best players, then everyone on the team would know it. Everyone would know that something was up, that their coach was not putting them in the best possible position to win the game. I wasn't going to be a party to that. So while I don't remember the exact game, at some point Texas Western became the first team to start five black players.

A funny thing happened. Nothing. Well, nothing more than what had happened before. The game went off, but there were no extra hisses or boos. If letters came in the next week, it wasn't much more than before. At least not enough to make the game stick out. We were still TWC, way out there in dusty El Paso, and there were only so many redneck racists who cared. If we had been the University of Texas or the University of North Carolina, maybe it would have become an instant national story, but we were Texas Western. Hell, it wasn't like we were on ESPN, but after that ball went up in the air I hardly ever thought about it again.

Unless someone asked me about it—and almost no one did until after the 1966 championship—it never even dawned on me. I certainly didn't think I deserved a medal or anything. All I had done is exactly what a coach is supposed to do; I started my five best players in an effort to maximize the chances of winning the game. To me they were just kids in white-and-orange uniforms. Not white guys, not black guys, just Miners. In later years I coached Hispanics, Native Americans, and foreign players. To me, they were all the same. They were my players. I certainly wasn't trying to make a social statement. I just wanted to win. If my five best players were from Mars, I would have started five Martians.

Now that I think back, it wasn't much different than when I was a high school coach and in charge of both the girls and the boys. Everyone assumed I would care only about the boys' team. It was common to favor them, work with them, push them, and coach them. But when it came to the girls, you just had gym class, got them to run around a little, and that was it. Who cared? Girls' basketball wasn't much back then, but I didn't see the difference. A team was a team. Players were players, white or black, male or female. I was in charge of the team and our goal was to win games. Why would I care about anything else?

So while some people have made me out to be a racial pioneer, I think my days coaching girls' basketball prove that I wasn't. I was just a coach who hated to get his ass beat and would do anything to avoid it. Play anyone, recruit anyone, work with anyone.

Years later people would refer to our national championship game against the University of Kentucky as the Brown v. Board of Education of college athletics, the linchpin moment that broke the color barrier for good. I always laughed at that. It was only big because we won. What if we had lost? In a lot of ways though, it did break the color barrier because the pressure on the southern schools that discriminated against black athletes was too great for them to continue to field segregated teams because we were now beating them on the court. Winning is more important than racism to some people. To me, I guess the real Brown v. Board of Education decision came one night with almost no one watching when faced with a simple question I made an easy decision.

I played my best players.

At the time, the last thing I expected was it would become a big deal. At the time I just wanted to win that game. Although, honestly, I don't even remember which game it was.

NINE

THE PIPELINE

Trying to recruit a team requires a delicate balance of talent and character. Get too much of one and not enough of the other, and it all falls apart. For Don Haskins's assistant coaches through the years, this posed a consistent problem. The definition of character is fluid. Haskins's definition wasn't. Even as late as the mid-1980s the ultra-stubborn, ultra-old school Haskins refused to sign a player with an earring or a tattoo, which to him just seemed like a sure sign of trouble.

Of course, talent is the mother of change.

"In 1986 we go to recruit a guy, Jerry Jones, in Chicago," said Tim Floyd, Haskins's assistant from 1977–86, who would go on to coach in the NBA. "It was before tattoos were a big thing and Jerry had one and Coach didn't know he had one. I hadn't dared to tell him because he never would have come on the recruiting trip if I had. Sometimes you had to trick him to recruit a guy. We pulled up to the gym outside Country Club Hills High School and I say, 'Hey, Coach, there are a couple of things I have to tell you about this guy.'

"He said, 'Oh, hell, here we go again. Why didn't you tell me this in El Paso.' And I said, 'Coach, Jerry is a good kid but he has a tattoo on his arm with his initials in the middle of a basketball.' He said, 'Well, let's just turn around and go back to the airport, we don't need a guy like him on our team.'

"So I said, 'Coach, it's barely recognizable. We're here, we might as well go in. Maybe we'll see someone else we like.'

"So we go in, and they are playing pickup and our guy Jerry comes down the court and dunks one so hard the backboard is shaking. Then down the other end he blocks a shot, runs back up the court, and dunks another one. He is six foot seven, 240 pounds and I can tell Coach is getting excited about his ability. Afterwards we were driving back to O'Hare and I said, 'Coach, what did you think of that tattoo on Jerry's arm?'

"And he said, 'Hell, I never even noticed it.' "

■

When you go to recruit a player, you think maybe you are getting one thing, but until they play for you, you can't be one hundred percent certain about anything. The second Bobby Joe Hill was the quickest guard I'd ever seen. He was from the Highland Park section of Detroit, a real tough area of the city. He was at Burlington Junior College in Iowa in 1964 when I first saw him play. His team had reached the junior college national tournament and I loved him. He was the Allen Iverson of his time. In the open court you could not stop him. If he was comin' right at ya, the quickest way he'd go around you was by whipping the ball behind his back going one way or the other. He'd just leave the defender flat-footed.

This is where I had to learn a little about coaching. While that style of play might work on the playgrounds of Detroit or for junior college ball, I wasn't sure it would work in college basketball or in my system. My assistant coach was Moe Iba, Mr. Iba's son; disciplined basketball was all either of us knew. Bobby Joe's dribbling would really bother Moe. He was saying every day, "Coach, he's a hot dog. He's a hot dog." Well, knowing Moe's dad, what could you expect? And I agreed.

So Bobby Joe's first year, 1964–65, I kept trying to get him to play under control. So I made him dribble the ball in front of him, like a crossover instead of his preferred between his legs. Well, he tried, but he kicked the ball away about half the time. He got frustrated, but he accepted it. He never bitched, never complained. That is the kind of character Bobby Joe Hill had. It was my fault he was struggling because I was overcoaching him. We could have been a helluva lot better that year if I just let him play a little bit.

The worst part of all of this was that we had a group of fans led by Bert Williams, who would later become our mayor, and he would boo Bobby Joe sometimes. According to Bert, they booed "because Bobby Joe wasn't playin' the way he could play." Instead he was tryin' to play the way I wanted him to play, which was the wrong way. It hurt our team because I took away the things that he could do. It was my fault. I had never had a player booed before and I would go crazy when I heard it in old Memorial Gym. I gave Bert hell for years for that.

So before the 1966 season I called Bobby Joe into the office and I said, "I want you to get the ball down the floor the best way you know how, and I want you to play just like you've always played." He sat over my desk and started grinnin'. I'll never forget what he said then: "Coach, everything is going to be OK now." And it was. He became the Bobby Joe Hill who would dominate basketball games. After I loosened up on Bobby Joe, all we heard were cheers. I asked Bert later, "Well, what happened to all them damn boos?"

I had high hopes because that was the year we had David Lattin in the program. I had recruited Lattin out of Worthington High School in Houston two years before. I had seen him play in a state tournament game. He was big, strong, powerful, and athletic, about six foot six and just a tough SOB. He was the next "Bad News" Barnes and I told him that. I showed him all of the records Barnes had set and he looked at them and said, "I'll break them." Well, I just loved that. When he and Bad News played in a pickup game it was a hell of a battle. I also loved that Lattin's high school team won the state tournament that year. I have always thought a winner is a winner. So I wanted Lattin and I tried, and tried, and tried to sign him out of high school. I made repeated trips to Houston and called him so much on the phone that to this day, almost forty years later, I can still remember the number to his mother's old house. I thought I was going to get him until he informed me of his demand.

It was giving a scholarship to the other "cats" at Worthington High. He wanted me to take the other four starters along with him. Well, the other guys couldn't play a lick, so I told him to forget it. No coach in his right mind would do that. I no longer loved that high school team anymore. I only wish I had known about the demand sooner so I wouldn't have wasted my time. As it turns out though, it wasn't a waste. David went to Tennessee State, but after a semester he was miserable. One night my home phone rang at 3:00 A.M. I heard, "Coach, this is Dave." I was half-asleep and a little pissed off. "Dave who?" I said.

"David Lattin," he said. "Coach, send me a plane ticket and I'll come to Texas Western. I want to come and play for you. Just send me the ticket." Well, hell, that was against NCAA rules, you are not allowed to provide transportation of any kind, plane, bus, even pick him up and drive him across town, for a transfer to your campus. He had to find a way there on his own dime. I had never even thought of doing something to break the rules, but this one sure tempted me for about a second. One plane ticket and I get David Lattin? That didn't seem like a big deal. But it was illegal and I quickly told him so. I also probably didn't have the money. "I

can't do it, David. You'll have to find a way here yourself."
I hung up and tried to go back to sleep, but that one hurt. I
think I dreamt of David Lattin for the rest of the night because he was so good. I tried to forget it though. David was in
Tennessee, probably broke, and that is a long way from El
Paso. The next college coach he called was sure to give him a
plane ticket. The next night I am sleeping again and the
phone rings at 5:00 A.M. "Coach, this is Dave again." Well, I
am half-asleep and more than a bit frustrated at this entire or-
deal so I snapped at him. "David, I cannot send you a plane
ticket. It is against NCAA rules . . ." He cuts me off. "Could
you pick me up at the Greyhound bus station in El Paso? I am
here. I came by bus." He had taken a bus straight through, for
twenty-four hours. Let me tell you, you never saw someone
get dressed quicker than I did that morning. It turns out (as I
would find out many years later) that just picking David up in
downtown El Paso and driving him a few miles to campus
was violating one of the NCAA's more questionable rules—I
guess he was supposed to hitchhike from the bus station—but
I didn't think of it at that moment.

At that point I had only one concern about Lattin—I
thought he would be difficult to coach. He was a big, tough
guy, with a cool Fu Manchu. His nickname was Big Daddy D.
I thought he would be a hell-raiser, a partyer, and a big drinker.
I figured I'd be draggin' his ass back from Juarez every weekend. He looked like trouble. He wasn't. Not even close. To this
day I don't think he has ever had a drink or a smoke. He has
always been a health nut, watching what he eats. Even now at

age sixty he looks terrific. He even wanted to play himself in the movie *Glory Road*. He was in good enough shape to do it, but I don't think he could pass as a twenty-one-year-old anymore. Lattin turned out to be a dream to coach. He had a lot of interests outside basketball and had a real popular campus radio show called "The Big D Jazz Session." I once asked him if he had any bad habits at all and he smiled and said, "Chasing babes." I laughed. I could live with that one.

If you thought I was excited when Lattin showed up, you should have seen me watching him practice during the 1964–65 season. NCAA transfer rules require a player to sit out one full season, meaning he can practice with the team but not play in the games. So David's focus and effort was on practice. He was beatin' up on everybody, although I didn't think he was playing as hard as he possibly could. He always told me he was. Then I found out the truth. The thing about that team was that they loved to play, but they hated to practice. I had to fight those guys every day—especially the next year—to practice hard, but they would play all day. I ran some brutal practices, but if they had a day off, they'd get three-on-three games going for fifty cents a game and have intense battles.

The first time I discovered these money games I came out of my little ole office over at Memorial Gym. It was a Sunday and I had given them their first day off in about two, three weeks. I heard a ball bouncin' in the gym. The one thing I'm not expectin' them to do was play some ball, but there they were with a three-on-three game goin'. I can still see this one play. Lattin missed a shot from the outside and it bounced back just above the free-throw line. He ran and grabbed it, took one step, jumped off his left foot, and went in for a dunk. He threw it down so hard he tore the damn rim off the backboard. As it was hanging down, Lattin slammed his arm against it and cut himself. He was bleeding all over the floor. And Andy Stoglin, who had tried to take a charge, had a Spalding logo on the back of his head and had gotten knocked cold by colliding with Lattin. I thought Andy broke his damned neck. Anyway, they all collapsed on the floor, with the rim hanging, blood flowing, and all the other players scattering. It was the damndest thing I had ever seen.

I came running in, piled Andy and David in my truck, and took them both to the hospital. Once I got everyone to the doctor I started getting pissed off. I had never seen Lattin play that hard, although I had suspected he was capable of it. The reason for the tenacity was the fifty cents. He would play harder for some cheap money game than he would for me. A lot of times our practices would run an hour longer than they were supposed to because I was so mad at Lattin and Bobby Joe. They'd rather take a whippin' than practice hard. Normally, your best players are your best practicers. But Bobby Joe was the only player I've ever seen who would not practice hard and then go out and get a bunch of guys together and play their asses off.

Bobby Joe was just stubborn. Once he got something in his head, it was staying there. I guess he was a little like his coach. During the 1964–65 season I sat Bobby Joe out of two games. I had told him to bring me his report card. I knew he wouldn't do it, not because he was defiant, but because his mind fluttered around. He'd just forget. Bobby had an IQ of 130 or something, but he would get only whatever grade he needed. If he needed an A, he got an A. If he needed a C, he'd get a C. So I told him, "If you don't bring me that report card you are sitting for two games." I put myself in a box because he forgot again and I had to sit him. That's not good coaching. You should never box yourself into a decision. One of the most stubborn mistakes I ever made was during that same year. I was tired of guys coming late for pregame meals, especially Bobby Joe Hill. He had my ass so chapped that I finally told the team, "The next player who shows up late is kicked off the team. Gone. Cut. No appeals. I don't care who it is." Think that is a bit severe? Well, the guy who shows up late is a kid named Jimmy Holmes, who was from El Paso and had never once been on my bad side. Just a great kid and a great student. Bobby Joe is there ten minutes early and Jimmy Holmes is late. He even had a good excuse for being late, he was in class. But I had boxed myself in and I kicked him off the team anyway. I almost reneged on that, but I had vowed that I would not put up with that crap anymore. That was over forty years ago and to this day I feel bad about that. It was bad judgment. But maybe Jimmy learned something about judgment from me. He graduated, went to law school, and wound up becoming a judge. So I was learning as a coach too.

One of the keys to recruiting our championship team was a man named Hilton White. He coached in the playground leagues up in New York City and was just a class guy.

Hilton had served in the Army and was stationed at Fort Bliss, which is in El Paso, so he knew the area. He knew that a black man could be treated fairly in El Paso, which just wasn't the case in many places across the country. When he had coached Willie Brown before Willie went to junior college I got to know him. Hilton was based out of the South Bronx and he had a ton of a great players he had taught on the playgrounds, all looking for schools. The kids all loved Hilton and if he said, "This is where you are going to school," well, that was where they were going to school. When I recruited Willie Brown I didn't know Hilton that well, but once I did right with Willie, I was in. Willie told me to keep calling Hilton White. "Coach," he said, "Hilton will get us all the players we want." I talked to him and he told me he would help get me players on one condition: I would make sure they were given a fair chance at an education. I told him no problem.

Hilton was always in my corner. When most of his guys got to El Paso they quickly hated me. I am sure all of them wanted to head back to New York, but Hilton would always take my side in an argument. He would tell them they needed to stay put, listen, and work harder. A lot of guys would have pampered their players and sent a plane ticket. Not Hilton. He wanted what was best for his players, and what was best was getting that education.

Hilton clued me into a five-foot-six guard named Willie Worsley. My first inclination was not to recruit a player who was five foot six, but I trusted Hilton. It was a good call. Worsley was so quick with the ball he could change the pace of the game. He was such a great athlete that despite his height he could dunk, which meant he could play bigger than his size. Worsley was from the Bronx as were two of his teammates, Willie Cager and Nevil Shed. The funny thing is that I never saw these guys play before they arrived on campus.

Recruiting was a bit suspect then. You had to take recommendations without ever seeing guys play. The only way to see a kid really play was to watch a high school game, but we didn't have the money to fly to New York. It is a long and expensive trip there now. Back in the 1960s there were fewer flights, the planes were slower, and tickets more expensive. Forget it. One trip to New York would chew up about a third of my recruiting budget, so there was just no way I could go. Besides, I never missed a game or a practice to recruit. As a result, you had to have connections. Later, after we won the NCAA title, I would make one trip a year to New York in the spring to recruit. I marvel now at our coaching staff at UTEP, led by Doc Sadler. Those guys recruit and recruit and recruit. They are almost never in El Paso, but that is the only way nowadays.

When Willie Brown called me to tell me about two guys from his neighborhood who were looking for a school, I listened. Willie Brown knew basketball. When I called Hilton and he recommended them too, I took them. It was a bit unusual. First off, not only did Willie Cager not play high school basketball, he hadn't gone to high school. He had worked and gotten his diploma by going to night school. That might scare off some coaches, but not me. He was helping his family and I liked his perseverance in getting his diploma. He had never played organized ball, just on the playgrounds where he was a local legend who everyone called Scoops. I offered Cager a scholarship and never regretted it. The only hitch in the plan was that in order to get admitted to Texas Western, Cager had to take two college-level English classes. He had no money, so he came to El Paso and found a job in town working while going to class. He didn't have enough for rent either, but we had a booster named Bob Brennan, who owned a service station down on Mesa Street in El Paso. Willie got a cot set up in one of the grease pits—right under where you pull your car up to get the oil changed. When the shop was closed, he slept in there until he passed those classes and we could get him on scholarship and move him into the dorm. Is that unbelievable or what? You think I had any doubt this guy was hungry?

His friend was Nevil Shed, a long-armed six-foot-eight forward who was a great defensive player. They wound up calling him the Shadow. Or, knowing Shed, he may have called himself that. I never saw Shed play before offering him a scholarship either. Shed was at North Carolina A&T, but was going to transfer. I was really concerned about taking him. Willie Brown had told me that Shed was leaving because he thought the coach at A&T was too tough on him. Hell, what was I going to be then? But Willie and Hilton both told me Nevil could make it in El Paso. I trusted Willie and then, to cap it off, I called Nevil's mother in New York City on the phone. She was a great woman—tough as nails. She wanted Nevil to get a diploma and to call her if he gave me any problems and it would be taken care of. Nevil was rightfully afraid of his mother. I'll tell you, as a coach, if every parent could be like Mrs. Shed life would be easy. Most parents want to know why their kids aren't playing more or why you are being so mean to them. Not Mrs. Shed. She saw the incredible opportunities basketball could give her son—sadly, it was rare that a black kid got to attend college back then. After talking to Mrs. Shed, the decision had been made. He and Cager showed up a little while later.

My New York pipeline was flowing, although later Shed would tell me that going to Texas Western College wasn't exactly considered the coolest thing in the neighborhood. I don't think too many people in New York had even heard of our school or El Paso. Shed told me he and Cager would wear their TWC gear on trips home and all the guys would call it Texas Women's College or Tiny Weenie College. Pretty funny. Shed said he got the last laugh though. Everyone knew what TWC stood for when we won the national title.

One quick word about Willie Brown. When Willie showed up on campus for the first time I immediately told him to shave off his mustache. I was concerned he didn't have enough discipline. Boy, was I wrong. Willie turned out to be one of my favorite players, and a great friend. He became a successful account executive at UBS Financial Services, Inc. in New York and did very well in life. College sports can change lives: I don't think the public gets reminded of that often enough. Consider Willie. Basketball got him out of New York, got him an education, and changed not just his life, but the life of his family. The players who go on to the

NBA are the ones who make millions and get the media attention, but it's the education so many of us (myself included) get while playing college sports that's invaluable.

Willie Brown and Hilton White had their own lives, careers, and families. They didn't need to spend their time calling around the country trying to send players to El Paso or wherever else, but they did. There were a lot of guys just like them. Scouting was so primitive and scholarships so valuable. Since many schools in the country wouldn't recruit black players, someone had to help these kids in their neighborhood. Someone had to be the go-between. Willie Brown got his big break, a college education. He knew it. He appreciated it. So he was spending his free time helping the next generation of guys who were just like him. Good kids who just needed a chance and could use basketball as a way out.

I get a lot of attention for being the first to start five black players in a game, but if it weren't for all of the leaders in the black community who helped send these kids to me it never would have happened. There are countless heroes in this tale and I thank all of them, even if they sent their players to someone else. This wasn't about just winning basketball games. This was about helping these young men, helping entire communities.

Willie and Hilton White weren't my only recruiting contacts. I had a friend named Jack Hobbs, who had played for Mr. Iba at Oklahoma A&M. When I was a freshman Jack was a senior. Jack became a high school coach in Gary, Indiana, a tough industrial city just outside of Chicago. One day Jack called me out of the blue and said he had seen a couple of players in the city. He didn't coach them and hardly even knew them, but he had scouted them. Orsten Artis was six foot one and quick as a cat. Jack told me he was a tremendous shot, a terrific rebounder for his size, and could really guard people. Jack played for Mr. Iba so he knew defense. I said I was interested. I got a little skeptical when I heard about the other guy, a six-five forward named Harry Flournoy. Jack said he was a real raw player who was probably a better musician and had been in the school band. But after Harry's junior year he decided to concentrate on basketball and quit the band. He averaged only three points a game, but Jack told me, "Don, you are not going to be impressed with his numbers, but Harry will be a hell of a rebounder."

It was after the 1962 season that I flew up to Gary to visit with Jack and see these potential recruits. I wanted to see just how good a shooter Artis was, so we had a free-throw shootin' contest. He claims he won, but I know that isn't the case. Not that it mattered, he was good. I offered him a scholarship on the spot. Harry Flournoy was a bit more difficult. Jack and I found him walking home from school for lunch. I pulled up beside him, asked if he was Harry Flournoy, introduced my-self, and asked if he wanted a ride. He said he didn't. I kept trying to get him in the car, but there was no way a black teenager was getting into a car with two strange white men in those days. Harry just wouldn't do it. I drove along real slow, talking to Harry while he walked for a few blocks and then gave up. We drove to his house and waited for him. When I got there I met with his mother, Amy, a great woman. We hit it off right away and it was funny, she liked me so much she offered me the last piece of apple pie in the house. It was great pie, Amy could really cook. Just after I finished, in walked Harry, surprised to see us there in his kitchen. He sat down for lunch and I told him about Texas Western. Then he asked his mother for dessert. Amy said, "Harry, there is none left, I gave the last piece to our guest, Coach Haskins." You should have seen the look on Harry's face. I told you it was great pie. He was so mad at me that he wouldn't let me drive him back to school. After the pie incident I thought we would never sign him. But I kept trying, he walked the whole way back to school with me driving slowly, again talking to him about how great Texas Western was out the driver's side window.

That piece of pie almost did in my recruiting efforts since Harry actually had another offer, from Indiana State. He wanted to go because it was closer to home, but Amy Flournoy trusted me and told her boy he was going to El Paso. Like I said, I loved that woman, but I would have loved her even if he had gone to Indiana State. She was a real disciplinarian who valued education; so much so that once during Harry's freshman year I caught him ditching class and saw his grades were slipping, so I called her. I was hoping she would call Harry and read him the riot act, but she did one better. She flew down to El Paso. We didn't tell Harry she was there. I just called him into my office. He walked in, saw his mother, and then we both read him the riot act. He was scared straight. I don't think Harry ever skipped class again. And anytime he would do anything to get me angry, I would say, "Harry, do you want me to get your mother down here again?" That was all it took.

Thank goodness the media didn't cover recruiting like they do now. I would have been roasted in the press for signing a guy out of the school's band with a three-point-per-game scoring average. But it just goes to show you how important that stuff really is. Harry was raw as a freshman, but I never had someone work harder during the summer. When he returned as a sophomore, he was a really good player. He just kept getting better and better. Oh, how Jack Hobbs's scouting report was correct. Flournoy averaged 10.7 rebounds a game during the 1965–66 season. I'm not sure I ever had a better rebounder. He just had a nose for the ball; he was Dennis Rodman only without the tattoos and crazy hair. Artis, of course, was a tremendous scorer for us throughout his career, especially in big games when he always seemed to play his best.

I remember Jack came to the Final Four in 1966 and approached me at one point and said, "I told you those two could play." They sure could, which is why I felt so good entering that 1965–66 season.

TEN

1966 SEASON

West Texas has been good to Haskins except, it seems, when it came to business. Through the years he got involved in a bunch of side ventures, looking to make a buck, and they all ended about the same way. There were the times he drilled for oil and found nothing but dirt. There was a short run of Don Haskins' Black Eyed Pea restaurant. He even once considered buying into an ostrich farm.

His friends call him the smartest man they ever met, someone in possession of an uncommon amount of common sense. He knew how to read people, size them up, talk to them. He wasn't so good with business plans.

"Why don't you say 'not worth a damn'?" Haskins laughed, finding gallows humor out of lost money. "Which would be true."

Once Haskins became a lettuce farmer. They don't normally grow lettuce near El Paso, but a farmer friend named S. M. Davis convinced Haskins the high desert of southern New Mexico was perfect for it. The key to lettuce growing is it can't have a real rain hit it for something like seventy-seven consecutive days. "If there is a big rain, then you're out of business, the lettuce will rot," said Haskins.

Haskins sunk twenty-two thousand, five hundred dollars into a lettuce field, a good chunk of savings. He was never paid very much at Texas Western, which isn't the kind of big-name school that pays its coach well. For seventy-seven days and nights there wasn't a meteorologist on El Paso television who watched the weather closer. If Haskins heard distant thunder in the middle of the night, he'd spring out of bed and drive out to the desert to watch his lettuce. "Who knew farming was so stressful?" he said.

The good news for Haskins was it didn't rain hard on his field for seventy-seven days. He had a bunch of nice lettuce. The bad news?

"Bumper crop outside Fresno," he said. "Drove the prices down. I lost it all."

Years later, as we slowly drove in his GMC truck past that field outside of Canutillo, New Mexico, he shook his head at another doomed deal. It was hardly a surprise. As a businessman, he made a hell of a basketball coach.

"See, there is this thing, maybe you heard of it, supply and demand . . ."

Don Haskins, Oklahoma A&M College

Mary and Don Haskins, Oklahoma A&M College, 1949

Don Haskins with son Mark, going hunting in Benjamin, Texas, 1955

Some members of the first TWC team 1961–62
from left: Don Haskins, Major Dennis, Danny Vaughn,
Willie Brown, and Bobby Joe Hill (the first Bobby Joe Hill)

Willie Worsley (left)
and Willie Cager (above)

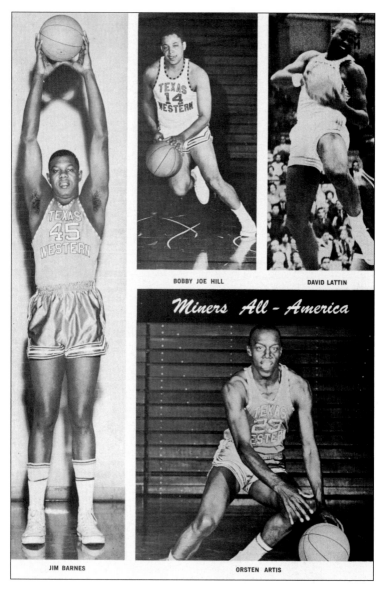

BOBBY JOE HILL   DAVID LATTIN

Miners All - America

JIM BARNES   ORSTEN ARTIS

Some prominent Miners

Head Coach Don Haskins and Assistant Coach Moe Iba

National Championship Game with Kentucky, 1966

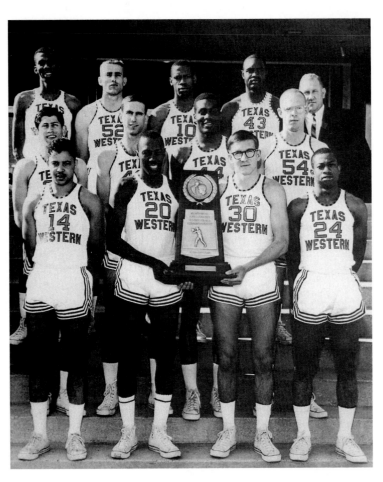

The 1966 National Champions, Texas Western College,
taken after the winning game

*Don Haskins
and Henry Iba*

*TWC Players
Reunion (from left):
Louis Boudoin,
Willie Cager, Harry
Flournoy, and
David Lattin*

*Don Haskins's induction to the
Basketball Hall of Fame, 1997*

Don Haskins enjoying retirement and a favorite pastime

All photos appear courtesy of Don and Mary Haskins.

■

When we started practicing for the 1965–66 season, I didn't know just how good we could be. The year before, we went just 18 and 9 and wound up in the NIT. Not bad, but not great either. I spent half the season worrying about Bobby Joe Hill, fighting with David Lattin to practice hard, and trying to get everyone to play together. This was easily the most talented team I had ever coached, but they were a pain in the ass when it came to practice. I had to fight them every damn day to do anything. Bobby Joe Hill would rather take a punch to the face than practice hard.

Then there was Lattin, who had the potential to be the best player in the country. I was always trying to do something to get Lattin jacked up. I always hated it when we played against a team with a white center. I would always get scared to death that Lattin wouldn't play hard because the center was white. He didn't think a white guy could play, so he didn't figure he needed to try his hardest. We never talked about it, but I could just tell. We'd be about to play some team the next night and he'd come by my office, "Coach, the dude, black guy or white guy?" I'd tell him white guy. And he'd say, "Aw, man."

One day Moe Iba and I were standing in the doorway outside of our office in Memorial Gym. You could see out onto the court from there. A maintenance man was in the gym cleaning up. He brought out a stepladder and started washing the backboard off. I said to Moe, "Let's play a little trick here." Moe ran into the office and got a little piece of tape. I gave the maintenance man a dollar and told him to tape it up well above the square on the backboard. It was way, way up there. Maybe fourteen feet up. You would have to be one hell of a high-riser to grab that dollar. Right then in walked David Lattin through a side door. He was in street clothes, but unlike a lot of college kids, he always dressed real nice, always was well groomed. He was Big Daddy D. The ladies loved him. He had on them Italian-lookin' shoes, you know, with no socks. He was cool. Well, that dollar caught his eye quicker than you can believe. "What's that?" And I said, "Anybody who can get it keeps it. Go put your clothes and your sneakers on, warm up, and we'll see if you can get it."

Lattin just smiled, walked over, and just hopped up there and picked it off the backboard. No warmup, in dress clothes and Italian shoes. He lands, puts it in his pocket, and keeps walking to the locker room. Unbelievable. It was a good thing the NCAA never found out about that trick, they probably would have taken away our national championship claiming I paid David Lattin. Anyway, Moe had this squeaky voice— everyone called him Squeaky—and he starts right in with me: "I told you, I told you! Lattin plays harder for money than he does for you." That was all the maddening proof we needed. When he wanted to, could he ever play.

Although the 1966 team was famous for having five black starters, and two good black reserve players, they weren't the only star players on the team. I had some very good white players, such as Jerry Armstrong, Dick Myers, David Palacio, Louis Baudoin, and Togo Railey. Togo was the fan favorite, a local guy who played only when we were up big. Late in the game the crowd would chant, "To-go, To-go," so I would put him in. He was my human victory cigar. But Armstrong, in particular, saw a lot of time because he was a good interior defender and a very talented player in his own right.

Our schedule that season didn't look too good. We had a few big games, but we were the overwhelming favorite for most. You have to understand, by that point no one would play us. We couldn't get any good teams to come to El Paso and challenge us. It just wasn't happening. We could play some games on the road, but even then coaches had begun ducking us. We had become a very good team in my five seasons and every coach in the country knew it. But their media, their boosters, and their school presidents didn't. We were still Tiny Weenie College from El Paso. If you are a major school such as the University of Michigan or Duke, why would you play us? The coach knew scheduling us was a no-win situation. If you win the game, everyone says, "Well, you are supposed to beat them, that's TWC." But if you lose, and with the team I had the odds were pretty good you weren't just going to lose, you were going to get your ass kicked, the critics would be all over you. "How could you lose to something called TWC?" So it was better just to avoid us completely. As a coach you were better off playing a weak team you were going to beat or another name team.

So getting games back then was brutal. This is one reason

we remained so unknown for so long. We weren't ranked high at the beginning of the 1965–66 season and we had never played back East in front of a lot of media. I knew we were really, really good though. I had played on Final Four teams at Oklahoma State. In 1963–64 I had a team with Jim Barnes that could have won it all. But my 1965–66 team was the best team I had been involved with. I just knew. Unfortunately, my players knew also and since a lot of the competition was weak, they didn't practice or play hard all the time to win.

The moment I knew we could really, truly play with anyone came during the annual holiday Sun Carnival Tournament that's held in El Paso every December. The people who ran the tournament had convinced Iowa to come down. This was a big deal because the Iowa Hawkeyes were ranked number four in the country at the time. Heading into the Sun Carnival Tournament we had won almost all our games easily. We were 8 and 0 and had played only one close game when we beat Fresno State 65 to 63. But the next night we played them again and won by eighteen.

In the opening game of the Sun Carnival Tournament we beat Loyola (of New Orleans) 93 to 56 to set up the matchup with Iowa the next night. The score looked good, but we stunk it up like we always did when we played an average team. When we played a team that wasn't very good my players just drove me crazy. We would guard somebody for maybe seven minutes each half and shut 'em out, and I mean just a total shutout. My guys could be so good on defense it was ridiculous. They just swallowed up other teams. Eventually, we would have this huge lead and they'd stop trying. We'd give up easy baskets and it would turn into playground ball. They'd be throwing crazy passes, taking wild shots and playing lackadaisical defense. I'd be going crazy on the sideline, allowing even a single easy basket would rip out my heart. But my players would just smile and look up at the scoreboard. We'd be up thirty, so why should I care? Well, I did. I thought you should play the game the right way for the full forty minutes and we weren't. We were so overconfident I knew we were fixin' to get our ass blistered in some game, I just didn't know when.

On the day of the championship game Moe and I were in a coffee shop in El Paso working on the scouting report and preparing a game plan. Ralph Miller, the Iowa coach, showed up with his team for a pregame meal. Coaches have different motivational tactics, they do it different ways. All the Iowa guys were settin' around this one table. I went over and told Ralph how good I thought his team was. And he said, "Yeah. We don't think we'll have a hard game until eight games down in the Big Ten." He said that right to my face and in front of his guys even though they were going to play us that night. I guess he didn't care about them being overconfident. I left with Moe soon after and I still couldn't believe it. We knew his players had heard everything. I was telling Ralph we were gonna have a hard game and he tells me and his team he doesn't expect it to be a hard game? I guess we just didn't get much respect back then.

We were on the verge of being in the top ten at that

point in the season, but I thought we were fixin' to get beat by Iowa because we weren't accustomed to giving a full forty-minute effort. I showed my guys the newspaper stories about Iowa being the quickest team in the nation and I'll tell you, that got their attention. I think they knew if they won the game they'd be in the top ten of the national polls. Every newspaper in the country ran the top ten of the Associated Press poll, so if we made it, Texas Western would appear in the newspapers back in New York, Detroit, and all their hometowns. So this was the perfect motivation. I think a lot of my players' friends and family back home didn't know how good we were. But being ranked would be proof. What-ever it was, I remember we even had a good practice the day of the game. Evidently, there had even been some talkin' the night before about which of the two teams was really better. Throw in the fact that Iowa would probably be overconfident and I was starting to feel better and better.

The first half of the game against Iowa was the best my team played all season and probably the best any team of mine has ever played. I remember the Shadow being so fired up about the game he was bouncing off the walls in the locker room just before the tip. We were all over them from the word jump. It was 14 to 0 before anyone knew it. Our guys were just suffocating on defense and that debate about who was the quickest team? Forget it. Iowa's first basket came only because Shed was so jacked up he mistakenly slapped the ball in our own basket. That was nine minutes into the game. At one point we led 34 to 4. So we wiped 'em out. Of course, from then on, what did we do? We didn't play a lick. The final score was 86–68. We had been ahead of them thirty points. We should have beaten them by thirty-five or forty. I wanted to hold their asses to forty. Hell, we gave up a ton of points and got outscored by three in the second half. Does that sound like a good effort?

This is what would drive me crazy about my players. A lot of people think it is hard for a team to keep up that level of play for forty minutes, but it isn't. We just never did. We would play in spurts. I had other teams that would play hard for forty minutes that weren't really as talented. If we had done that in 1964 we would have won the title, but we didn't. And we certainly didn't in 1966, even though we did win it all. This was maddening. So even though we crushed the number four team in the country, at home, in front of an overflow crowd, and set off all sorts of parties and jubilation in El Paso, I was sitting on the bench miserable. I just could not accept anything less than complete and total effort. No matter what the score was. I could never separate effort from the final result. To me the score wasn't as important as the way we played the game. I always tell folks that some of the teams of which I am proudest didn't even make the NIT, but they did maximize their talent and gave me everything they had.

The win over Iowa did get us some attention. We were in the top ten of the national polls, which was great for El Paso. People were really excited about our team. El Paso had no other sports teams then and really no national identity at all. There were a couple of old country songs about El Paso, but

I think most of the country thought it was located in Mexico. Which it damn near is. So the people of El Paso embraced something of their own and became Texas Western Miner fans. It was great. We had fans of all nationalities, people from Juarez across the border driving over for games. It wasn't just TWC students and alums. People who had gone to other schools, such as the University of Texas or the University of New Mexico, but lived in El Paso, got caught up in it, not to mention all of the people who didn't attend any college. It was the start of a love affair that continues to this day.

The fans were unbelievable when we first started winning and by 1965–66 their enthusiasm and support was out of control. We would go on the road, win a big game, and when we landed at the airport there would be two or three thousand people waiting for us. Even after a little game there would be hundreds. They would line up in the long hallways at the El Paso airport and shake our hands as we walked by. It made all of us feel like real road warriors. The players began to feel that they weren't just playing for themselves or their school, but an entire city.

My problem was gettin' them to play for me. They kept screwing around, playing half a game, getting a big lead, and then letting up late. There was the time at New Mexico we trailed by twenty-five with thirteen minutes left. I told them, "I knew it was gonna catch up with you." Then they turned it on and we wound up winning by three in overtime. No one wanted to listen to me; we were winning every game, often by double digits. There was nothing I could do. And I tried everything. I rode those guys like never before. I'd practice all night after a win. I'd holler and shout. I used to tell them I was going to buy them all skirts if they didn't toughen up. It didn't matter. It was an exhausting season because I had to fight this team so hard every single day. We had five players—Bobby Joe, Flournoy, Shed, Palacio, and Baudoin—who were left-handed. So maybe that explained it.

We went over to Arizona State in late January that season. Since half the guys were always on the verge of flunking out we always took a week or two off for final exams. We'd try to practice a little every day, but my main concern at that point was getting guys to pass and on their way to that diploma. I didn't want a bunch of bus drivers like I had been. We had a game right after exams at Arizona State. Ned Wulk was the coach and he had some good teams in the past, but this one wasn't that good. We should have been able to blow them out, but heck no, we were playin' along just like always, hard one minute, screwing around the next. It was a close game.

I called time-out, I was madder than hell. So I put them in the zone. I said, "Hill, you're here, Orsten you're here, Shed you're here." They went out to the middle of the floor and Hill gets 'em in a huddle. ASU had the ball and came down, but my guys didn't go into a zone like I said. Instead they stuck to man-to-man and got after them like you wouldn't believe. We defended like a pack of wolves, we were all over them. They didn't score a point for about seven or eight minutes, and we got our twenty-point lead. And Moe said, "Coach, Coach, they're not doing what you told 'em." I said, "I know, Moe, and I love it."

I put them in the zone because I knew they hated playing

zone. I was tryin' to piss them off because I was tired of watching them sit there and do nothin'. So they tried to piss me off right back by not playing zone, but playing the best man-to-man defense I'd ever seen. During those seven or eight minutes, they wiped ASU out. Of course, they went right back to doggin' it. This was the type of team they were. It was always something. Always a fight. It all comes from your guard. If you've got a guard who at half court will put pressure on the ball and stay between his man and the basket then everything gets easy. Playing defense is easy, really. All you have to do is stay between your man and the basket, and every time the ball moves, five players move with it. Sounds pretty simple, but it was hard to get them to do it. The way you learn to play defense is from practice, practice, practice. You have to practice so much that defensive adjustments become second nature: actions, not reactions. It comes only from repetition, and maybe from having some old man screamin' hour after hour about bending your back, moving your feet, and seeing the ball until the balls of your feet are about to fall off. To be successful at anything, people have got to develop good habits and then practice them over and over and over.

Playing defense this way forces the other team out of its comfort zone. Teams develop certain tendencies in their offense. I was convinced our defense was so good that it could force our opponents out of that comfort zone. You have to guard them in spots on the court they weren't used to being guarded in. We won a lot of games through the years by doing that very thing, even when we didn't have the best talent. A point guard is important here. If you don't have a guard that can do that, you're not going to have a real good defense. This is what I always believed, at least.

We were still undefeated, 23 and 0, when we took a trip to play Seattle on March 3 in the final game of the regular season. We had already qualified for the NCAA tournament, which was to start on March 6 in Wichita, Kansas. We had beaten Seattle 76 to 64 in El Paso, so my guys were overconfident and overlooking Seattle. But Seattle was a very good team. During the game Bobby Joe took the ball to the basket, leapt in the air, and got cut from underneath by a Seattle player. He went down hard and no foul was called. I was going crazy and then I heard the Seattle crowd shouting and it sounded like "Boo, boo." I couldn't understand it, they should have been happy there was no call. Well, Moe Iba tells me the official's name is Lou. They were shouting, "Louuu, Louuu." The stands were chanting the official's name. Damnedest thing I ever heard. They loved Lou there. And ole Lou took care of them pretty good, we didn't get a damned call all game. The next year we played at Seattle again and when I saw that SOB Lou walk into the gym I went nuts. I got called for a technical before the game even started.

But in that March 1966 game, forget it, Seattle beat us 74 to 72 and it wasn't just the official. After that game the last team in America I wanted to play again was Seattle. They were really good and had three or four black players. I would have rather played Kentucky five times in a row. This wasn't an all-white team, hell no. And that was still in the Elgin Baylor era, so basketball was big in Seattle. After that loss, our first of the season, I didn't want any part of those guys again. Besides, from the way we had played, like it was an exhibition game, we deserved to lose. Bobby Joe particularly frustrated me because he hadn't played up to his ability and was acting like a true leader on the court only in spurts. I demanded a great deal from him because he was so good and so important to our success. But too often he wasn't living up to my standards.

I was angry with my team so I set a curfew that night. We were going to fly out the next morning to Wichita, Kansas, for the NCAA tournament and I didn't want any crap that night. Well, Bobby Joe apparently knew some girls in Seattle and he and the rest of the team snuck out. Probably the only funny thing about the whole incident was finding Shed in his room. Once I realized some guys had snuck out already, I, of course, immediately headed to Shed's room because I figured that if there was trouble he was probably in the middle of it. I went crashing into his room and he was under the covers, looking at me with a smile, pretending like he was just trying to get some sleep. I was like, "What the heck?" If there was one guy I thought would have snuck out it would have been Shed. No way I was believin' this. He had the covers pulled up to his chin, a little suspicious, so I yanked the blankets off of him and there he is, fully dressed, shoes and all. I had caught him right before he left.

Angry doesn't describe me at that point. I was just so mad I couldn't help myself. The guys got back around 3:00 A.M. and I had left all their doors open so they knew they were busted. Then we woke them up at 4:30 A.M., claiming we had an early flight. So I had a bunch of tired players on the plane, but I told Moe Iba and our trainer, Ross Moore, to walk back and forth on the plane and if anybody even looked like he was about to doze off to go back and wake him up. I didn't want anyone sleeping. If I was too angry to sleep, then by God, I wanted them too angry to sleep. The fact they had been out all night was not a suitable excuse for taking a nap. I am sure my players weren't too happy with me at this point, but they were smart enough to shut up and take it.

We were about to enter the NCAA tournament with a 23 and 1 record and a national ranking of number three. Our team was one of the favorites to win the national championship. While I was upset by the Seattle loss and the guys breaking curfew, my mind went back to the Arizona State game just before Christmas when my team refused to play zone defense. A friend of mine named Dow Wigginton lived in Phoenix and attended the game. He had played for Mr. Iba at Oklahoma A&M so he knew basketball. I went over to his house after the game and had a few beers. While we were settin', he looked at me—and this was the first time I'd ever heard this—he said, "You know, those damn guys you have are something else. They play hard. You could win the whole ball of wax." I'll never forget it. It's the first time anyone said that to me. I'd already been thinkin' that in my mind. Like I said, I sometimes had a difficult time separating the reality of how good we were (really good) with my standard for good (something close to perfection). I knew we were better than I was letting myself admit.

But here is Dow Wigginton, who had played on teams good enough to win the national title, a fairly neutral observer, and he thinks we can win it all. The rest of the country was talking about Kentucky and Duke—they had a lot of media attention. But Texas Western, national champions? Dow thought so. And it was at that moment when I really started thinking so too. They may not be good enough to make me happy, but they're good enough to be better than every other team in the country: I still thought it on the flight out of Seattle.

As long as we didn't screw it up.

ELEVEN

THE NCAA TOURNAMENT

It was 1998 and Don Haskins was sixty-seven at the time. We were inside the Don Haskins Center, UTEP's 12,222-seat home arena. From the rafters hung dozens of banners commemorating his national and league championships. In a few minutes he was going for career win number 704. He was wearing a Rolex commemorating his enshrinement into the Naismith Basketball Hall of Fame.

He was his own man, a living legend, the king of west Texas, virtually beyond criticism from a fan base that worshipped his every move. Anytime he wanted to be mayor of El Paso, sixty-something percent of the electorate was waiting to vote for him. If there was ever a person who could not be fired, it was Don Haskins at this stage of his career.

But as he dressed for a UTEP home game, he pulled out a rather unusual garmet to make a rather unusual fashion choice for an even more unusual reason.

"A clip-on tie?" I laughed as Haskins struggled to get this ridiculous little blue thing attached to his white dress shirt.

Haskins shot me a look.

It was, indeed, a clip-on tie. I don't think Haskins owns a real tie. He hates dressing up at all, preferring an open collar with some room to breathe. The funniest part of the clip-on is that he would put it on only seconds before leaving the locker room to take the floor before a game, and by the time they called his name during the pregame introductions, he'd already have ripped it off and given it to a manager.

Haskins wore the tie for less than a minute each game, just long enough to take the court with an air of business sensibility.

"Mr. Iba told me before my first game as a high school coach always to wear a tie," said Haskins of his mentor, who had been deceased for a few years. "Administrators always like ties. You can take it off if the game gets hot, but always wear one at the start. Might help you if you get in a pinch."

I noted to him that the entire building was named after him and, in reality, the clip-on act wasn't exactly fooling anyone into thinking he was sharing a closet with Rick Pitino.

He didn't get my point.

"Mr. Iba said to wear a tie," he said, ending the discussion and straightening the clip-on.

■

I was so mad at Bobby Joe for the Seattle debacle, I benched him. I just said forget it, the guy screws around in a big game and then not only sneaks out after curfew, but takes the whole team with him. When I told him to be a team leader I sure wasn't talking about leading the team to a party. I had absolutely had it with him. By that point, I had tried everything. I ran him, yelled at him, and talked nicely to him. So this was it, I was benching him. He would not play at all in the next game. If we lost, so be it. I may have been the coach of the number-three-ranked team in the country (Kentucky was number one), but I was still a stubborn SOB. Bobby Joe knew enough to accept the punishment without saying a word. In the best of times, I wasn't the kind of coach a player talked back to and this was not the best of times.

But here is the rub. Our next game was in the NCAA tournament; if we lost, our season was over. We would play against a terrific Oklahoma City team, one of the best in the country, coached by Abe Lemons, himself one of the best in the country. Back in 1966, the NCAA tournament was set up regionally. They still do that today in name. There is the East Regional, the Midwest Regional, and so on. But nowadays UCLA is as likely to be in the East and Michigan State in the West as opposed to where you'd think they would be.

But not then. Teams from the east played in the East Regional. The west in the West Regional. Which is why we had such a tough draw. For whatever reason, the NCAA thought El Paso, Texas, was in the Midwest. They probably didn't even know where it was, so they just put us there. The Midwest was tough though. It meant we were in with the best teams from the Big Eight, the Big Ten, and the Missouri Valley, which were excellent in those days. And that meant instead of some cupcake team in the opening round—the way a 23 and 1 team would draw today—we got Oklahoma City.

Abe Lemons was a great friend of mine but he was like that with everyone. He was a very good coach and one of the funniest guys I've ever known to coach college basketball; I actually think his sense of humor overshadowed his coaching skill. Abe was from Oklahoma and grew up in the Dust Bowl era too. Abe wasn't even his name. It was actually just A.E. and the initials didn't stand for anything. He used to say he was born so poor he couldn't even afford a name. Eventually he added the B in the middle because, as he liked to say, "It's tough gettin' by as just initials."

He loved to nickname his players. On the 1966 team he had a big center named Charles Hunter, who he called Big Game. There was another guy named James Ware, a great rebounder, and Abe called him Weasel. Abe was always cracking jokes, doing crazy stuff. One time in a game a referee was just killing him with bad calls and Abe yelled to the guy, "Hey, Charlie, do me a favor, next time you come to town bring your wife." The ref said, "Why, Abe?" And Abe said, "Because then you'll have someone to screw other than me." When he was the coach at the University of Texas he attended a booster club meeting where a guy asked him about a coaching error he had made that cost the Longhorns a game. Abe asked the guy what he did for a living, and the guy said, "Doctor." Abe chuckled, "Well, you have it easy. You get to bury your mistakes."

Years later when he was at UT, he came over to El Paso to play in a golf tournament with me. It was me and Abe against two other guys and I'll admit that we had some action on the game. For two days Abe stunk. He couldn't make a shot, couldn't hit a putt. He just killed us. I was fuming. Part of it was because this was going to cost me, but mainly because I hated to lose in anything. We are sitting out on the fairway of the eighteenth hole, about to get our asses beat, and Abe said, "Don, let me make this up to you. Let me bring my Texas team over to El Paso this season for a game and then you can beat us in front of your home crowd." Well, that sounded good; getting a team such as the University of Texas to visit our arena would be great and my fans would certainly like to beat the Longhorns. But I got to thinking that I had read that UT was going to be in the preseason top ten. He could bring them over, but there was no way Abe would really throw the game. Since UT was so good they'd probably beat us. So that wasn't going to help me at all. Hell, he was probably trying to hustle me. I expressed this to Abe, who thought for a moment and then said, "Hell, to make it fair, I'll just bring my white guys."

But I wasn't in any laughing mood heading into the first round game with Oklahoma City. I knew how good Abe's

team was that year and I'd about as soon as played anyone but
them. To make matters worse, we were going to play without
Bobby Joe. As good as Lattin was, Bobby Joe was the key to
our team. I laugh now about the sensation it would make today if the coach of the number three team in the nation (a
number one seed nowadays) benched his star point guard for
the NCAA tournament. Hell, they'd be breaking in on ESPN
to talk about it. The media would be going nuts. Fans, talk radio, Internet message boards. You name it. Back then, nothing. No one even knew. It didn't even make the newspapers.

With no Bobby Joe, I knew Lattin would be the key. I
needed to get the big guy motivated so Moe and I went to
great extremes to convince him that we were playing against
the greatest rebounder in the nation, Weasel Ware. We told
him Weasel was going to get twenty rebounds on him and that
no one could stop the Weasel. Hell, by the time we were done
talking up the Weasel he was a combination of Wilt Chamber-
lain and Lew Alcindor. Then we told him that the coaching
staff from the University of Houston was going to be at the
game. Houston was playing Colorado State in the other game
that day—even though we wouldn't meet in the next round.
Lattin was from Houston and ever since he was a little kid he
wanted to go to UH. Even though UH had some black players, it didn't recruit him, so David always wanted to play well
in front of those UH coaches and stick it in their faces.

In practice we could never get Lattin to help on defense,
which was to switch off his man and defend anyone who got
near the basket. We just couldn't do it. But in the Oklahoma
City game, that SOB was like a cat out there. I had never seen

him play so intensely. Lattin got after the Weasel. Lattin had twenty points and fifteen rebounds. The Weasel had ten points and twelve rebounds, not bad, but nothing like he was used to getting. After the game, one of the UH assistants, Harvey Pate, told a newspaper that watching Lattin guard the Weasel was incredible. "I've never seen a guy scrape skin from the top of his head to his navel," Pate said. I think Lattin understood the significance of the game in a way our other guys didn't.

They had plenty to worry about because midway through the first half we were down around eight or ten points. I had told them Oklahoma City was pretty damned good, and now they were starting to believe it. To make matters worse, my team doctor, Joe Galatzan, was sitting down at the end of the bench hollerin' at an official something fierce for making a bad call. And all of a sudden the official gave my team doctor a technical. I couldn't believe it. My team doctor? I went down to the end of the bench to talk to him but I felt sorry for him. God, he was just a little bitty guy and was slumped down, all embarrassed that he had just hurt the team. Dr. Joe said, "Coach, I'm sorry." I said, "You didn't do a damn thing. I was fixin' to get one myself."

Anyway, I called time-out to regroup and I noticed Bobby Joe wasn't sitting back on the bench pouting, like a lot of guys would. We huddled up and even though he wasn't playing, Hill was right in the middle, grabbin' guys by the shirt, getting in their faces, shouting encouragement, even giving some advice on what he had seen.

I loved it. He was, after all, the leader of the team. It's hell to have a leader that won't play hard in practice and breaks curfew. But here he was, acting like a leader, he wasn't poutin'. Maybe I'm makin' an excuse for myself, but it was about seven minutes before halftime when I put him in. The benching was over. I was no longer mad about Seattle, I was mad that we were getting our asses beat by Oklahoma City. With Hill we went from being down eight or ten points to jumping up seventeen, just like that. Bobby Joe was unbelievable. He made everything happen on both ends of the court. You know, settin' on that bench, I think he saw everything that everyone was doing wrong. He was such a smart player. Instead of pouting he had studied the game. So once he got in the game, problems got solved. We won easily, 89 to 74.

After the game Abe came up to me and said, "If you had just left that damn Hill over there on the bench, we might have beat ya." Sorry Abe. The victory moved us into the second round of the tournament, leaving us two victories from reaching the Final Four and four from winning the national championship. When we flew home to El Paso, there was a huge crowd of fans waiting for us at the airport. It was unbelievable. They lined the hallways to welcome us home. It took about an hour just to get our bags. The city of El Paso was going crazy for us.

The next two games shifted to Lubbock, Texas, in the Coliseum. It was a building I knew and loved. In my entire career I never lost in the Coliseum, whether it was high school games with Hedley and Dumas, NCAA games, or anything against Texas Tech. We were going to play Cincinnati, which was another real good team then.

I was excited about playing in Lubbock because some of my old friends were able to come over and watch the game. Guys from Benjamin, Hedley, and Dumas. I remember going on the court before the game and looking over and there was this guy with a little black cowboy hat on, my friend Pate Menzer, with his son Wyman. I am still friends with Pate to this day. Pate came with a bunch of cowboys, old friends of mine from little Benjamin, they were all in blue jeans, cowboy boots, out of place at an NCAA basketball game. It was great.

Cincinnati was 18 and 4 and one of the most well-balanced teams we faced. That was a problem because they didn't have one star. I couldn't pull out a stat sheet or an All-American list to motivate my players. There was no Weasel and his twenty rebounds a game to talk about in order to get Lattin's attention. The Bearcats were just a bunch of selfless guys with modest stats who cared only about winning. This is a nightmare team for a coach to face.

Well, it didn't take long in the game before we started to get beat. Once again, we weren't playing defense with enough effort and UC was getting some easy baskets. We were just screwing around in the first half and I was so frustrated I sat back in my chair and I told our trainer, Ross Moore, "Mo, I'm glad this crap is over. I am sick and tired of it." With about seventeen minutes left we were still down about seven. We hadn't pissed a drop all game. By that I mean we hadn't done anything. Hill gathered the guys together and yelled at them, which is probably what saved us. He could do a lot more with 'em than I could. Sure enough, about eight minutes later

Cincinnati hadn't scored a point and we're ahead by seven. It was like flipping a switch. And then we screwed up again. One of their guys, Don Rolfe, a big ole white boy, knocked the crap out of Jerry Armstrong when Armstrong wasn't looking, but Nevil Shed saw him. The next time down the court Shed laid Rolfe out with a punch; he just let him have it. It was a cheap shot, but it was a retaliatory cheap shot. I think South Bronx playground standards call it justifiable assault. Shed got booted from the game. I was so mad at him, not because he had done it, but because he had done it at a critical juncture of the game and so I wouldn't let him sit on the bench. I sent him to the dressing room and told him he was off the team, scholarship revoked and everything. I was that angry.

The game went to overtime and we barely won it 78 to 76. We had been lucky. Willie Cager played really good defensively in Shed's place. Lattin got motivated and finished with twenty-nine points. I was sick after the victory, even though it was a victory. I think it was at that moment I knew I would never get these guys to play forty minutes of basketball the way I wanted them to. After the game, Shed came up to me crying. He was apologizing and begging and carrying on. He had called his mother from a pay phone and told her he was coming home, that he had been kicked off the team. He said his mother wanted to speak to me. I was in no mood to speak to anyone's mother, but I respected that woman so much that I did it. I was expecting her to beg for forgiveness, ask for Nevil to get a second chance. Most parents will automatically defend their children. His mother got on the phone and says, "Coach, make that boy walk home. Make him walk back to New York. Don't even give him a ride to the bus station." Well, how can you throw a guy off the team with a mother like that? She was the best. She was angrier at Shed than I was. So I decided then and there to keep him on the team. I figured I was saving him from the whipping of his life. I did bench him for the start of the next game though.

You know, a lot is made about how my team had seven black players and five of them started, but black and white wasn't that big of a deal to us. On our team, as far as I knew then or have ever heard, there were no racial problems, no divisions. Jerry Armstrong was white and when he got hit with a cheap shot, Nevil Shed, who was black, didn't hesitate to stick up for him. It wasn't about race with us. They were all teammates. While I am sure my players dealt with some racism outside of the team, I wasn't aware of it. Not in El Paso and not on the road. Race just wasn't a topic that was brought up by the team. We just played basketball.

The regional final was in Lubbock the next night and we played the Kansas Jayhawks. This would go down as one of the greatest games in the history of the NCAA tournament. Kansas was led by two All-Americans, JoJo White, a guard, and Walt Wesley, a great seven-foot big man. We pointed Wesley out to Lattin about every waking minute. There was almost no time to prepare and back then we didn't have any scouting budget, so all we had to go on was what Moe Iba and I saw when we watched their previous game. Kansas was the best team we played that year. Better than Kentucky. Better than Seattle. Whoever won this game was going to win the national championship. If KU had beaten us, they would have won it all.

Because the game came up so quickly, the day after our victory against Cincinnati, there wasn't much buildup. These days there is a lot of hype surrounding the NCAA tournament, but back then you just played. Our guys weren't nervous or anything. The game was a back-and-forth affair. Our guys respected Kansas from the start because they had two All-Americans and we could just tell they were a really good team. We had a three-point lead in the final minute of the second half, but JoJo White hit a bucket, was fouled, and calmly hit the free throw to force overtime, 69 to 69. Then at the end of the first OT, with the score tied at 71, White threw in a jump shot right at the buzzer. On television it looked good, but he had a foot on the out-of-bounds line and the basket got waved off. It was the right call, but this is how close we came to losing. We pulled ahead in the second overtime thanks to a put-back by Cager, and Shed hitting a couple free throws, which succeeded in getting him firmly out of my doghouse. In the end we hung on for the 81 to 80 victory to send us to the Final Four. The key to the game was our defense. Lattin and Shed did a great job on Wesley. He finished with twenty-four points and fifteen rebounds, but he went just nine of twenty-three from the floor. Those two made him earn it. Lattin got his also. He had seventeen points and fifteen rebounds. It was just an incredible game.

Did I say there was a big crowd of fans at El Paso International when we came back from beating Oklahoma City? Well, that was nothing compared to the throng that met us the day after making the national semifinals. Thousands of people were there, waving signs, clapping, taking pictures all the way from the gate to the baggage area. I got off the plane at 11:00 A.M and I got to my car at 3:30. I was a guy who tended to have tunnel vision about things, but I understood that this was one of the biggest things ever to happen to El Paso. Our city just doesn't get much national attention and back then it was even smaller. Which is why the whole city was behind us, a feeling I can't describe, but am humbled about to this day.

But I couldn't get too emotional. We were two games from winning it all. The competition was about to heat up. And so was the attention on our starting five.

TWELVE

THE FINAL FOUR

"I answered the phone one morning in the office and a man was looking for Coach Haskins," said Tim Floyd of a day in the mid 1980s. "I told him Coach wasn't in and the man said he was the mayor of Van Horn, Texas, and he wanted to thank Coach personally for what he did for a couple of his residents.

"I hadn't heard a word about it so I asked what the story was. The mayor said a young Mexican family, husband, wife, three kids, were driving from Van Horn to Los Angeles, looking to start a better life. They didn't get far before their car broke down on the side of the road out in the desert. Coach was out hunting and he stopped to *help. He realized this family had no money, so he got a tow truck to bring the station wagon to El Paso and loaded the whole family into his truck. He then paid for the tow, paid to get the car fixed, and since it took two days for the work to be done, put the family up in a motel and gave them cash for food.*

"I couldn't believe it. All of that for some family he never met. I called Mary Haskins and asked if Coach had mentioned it to her. She said, no, she had no idea. So not only did he do all of that, he didn't tell a soul about it. Not one person. He didn't want anyone to know. He didn't want any credit.

"He came into the office the next day," Floyd said, "I asked him about it. He just shrugged."

■

Utah was the champion of the West region and our opponents in the national semifinals. Duke and Kentucky would meet in the other semifinal, which attracted the most fan and media attention because those were the two storied programs. Almost everyone figured the winner of the Duke-Kentucky game would go on to win the national championship. That was fine with me, they could believe whatever they wanted.

The Final Four that year was in College Park, Maryland, in Cole Fieldhouse on the campus of the University of Maryland. Cole is a great building, an old-fashioned basketball barn up on top of a hill in the middle of campus. The Final Four has gotten so big these days that it is quaint to think of the NCAA holding it on an actual college campus. Now they don't even play the games in a basketball stadium, but converted football domes. Heck, back then they didn't even call the Final Four the Final Four, but it was still a big deal. The Washington, D.C., area was into the games and there was more media there than I had ever seen. I later heard an interesting story about that Final Four. A kid named Gary Williams was a sophomore guard at Maryland then and he snuck into Cole Fieldhouse to watch all the games. He said he marveled at our team. Gary would, of course, go on to be a great basketball coach at Ohio State and then Maryland, where in 2002 he won the national championship himself. I always respected the way his teams played—tough both mentally and physically, and very aggressive defensively—and I got a kick out of hearing that story.

The week before the game against Utah the racial makeup of our team began getting a lot of attention. That week Frank Deford of *Sports Illustrated* called me for an interview, and in previewing the games in the magazine he wrote: "All seven of the Texas Western regulars are Negroes, hardly a startling fact nowadays but one that becomes noteworthy because of the likely meeting with Kentucky or Duke. Both those teams are all-white. It is unfortunate—but it is a fact—that some Ethniks, both white and Negro, already are referring to the prospective national final as not just a game but a contest for racial honors."

Oh, brother. I have nothing against Deford, he is a great

writer and it was an obvious storyline, but all the East Coast media that didn't know anything about ole Texas Western now knew one thing about us: We had a bunch of black guys starting. I don't know who or what "some Ethniks" were, but it sure as hell didn't include anyone associated with my team. You can ask my players to this day and they will tell you that while they were obviously aware that we had black guys and Duke and Kentucky didn't, it wasn't that big of a deal to us at that point. Again, I think they spent too much time hating me and screwing around in an effort to piss me off to care about that. But the media made a big deal of it. And I guess I understand why.

Personally the black player I was most concerned about didn't even play for me. It was Jerry Chambers of Utah, a great player. If we didn't figure out a way to stop him then we were never going to get to play for "racial honors," or whatever the hell *Sports Illustrated* was talking about.

I had one advantage though. The Utah coach was Jack Gardner, and he was one of the best offensive coaches in the game. He was the master of what they later called the fast break. I knew he had a bunch of great drills for pushing the ball up the court that I wanted to see and use. So during the fall of that year I had called him and asked if I could come and watch practice one day. This is a fairly common thing for coaches to do; I hosted scores of guys through the years. He was a terrific guy and said yes. Who knew we'd wind up playing in the national semifinals? The Texas Western football team was playing at Utah so I gave my guys that Saturday off and flew up and back with the football team. His drill was great. It was a five-on-two fast-break drill where his guys went just about everywhere. It was very confusing for the defense, but the moves were fairly scripted. In the drill, the two defensive guys getting back were just dummies, they didn't actually try to guard anyone. The drill was about getting the flow of the fast break down, it was designed to help the offense. It was incredibly effective too—Utah made the semifinals despite losing three regulars to injuries that year.

Well, the Mr. Iba in me saw this drill and got to thinkin' about flippin' it around. Instead of coming back with a five-on-two fast-break drill, I came back with a two-on-five defensive drill. I had two guys gettin' back down the court, but instead of just standing there watching the offensive players run by them, they had to guard everyone. I made everyone do it, even the big guys who, because they would normally be fighting for rebounds, would in all likelihood never be the two back on a fast break. What we did was work on stoppin' the ball, always getting somebody to guard the basket. We constantly worked on getting back defensively. This was a hell of a drill and it really helped our transition defense throughout the season. And now that we were going to play Utah, it was really a hell of a drill. My guys were so used to getting blitzed by a five-on-two fast break that if it ever happened in a real game they were prepared. Utah's big advantage was something we had been inadvertently practicing against the entire year. Jack Gardner knew this and before the game he said I had an advantage because I got to watch him practice.

Jack actually got to watch us practice also though. The day before the semifinal game all four teams had an open practice at Cole Fieldhouse. The crowd consisted of media, diehard fans, and other college and high school coaches hoping to glean some information. They still do it to this day. With a crowd watching, the practices are usually lighthearted affairs. Just some getting loose time, getting the jitters out, getting guys used to the rims and the backdrop of wherever you are playing. A lot of coaches will have a second private practice at a local gym where they will install the game plan. Who would think to practice for real, after all, in front of thousands of people, including the other coach?

Me, that's who. What did I know? I was just never the kind of guy who could have a half-ass practice or put the guys through some show drills. Something would inevitably piss me off and I would get deathly serious. I was so aggravated that entire weekend anyway it didn't take long for me to lose it. From the media, to my team's lack of concentration, to a stomachache that I had the entire time, everything seemed like a constant hassle. We started the practice and we were out there just goin' through the motions like we were playin' the season opener. I got so damn mad at 'em. I was embarrassed. There were a lot of people out there, all my peers, the media, and we are practicing like crap. We were running a couple of defensive drills and Bobby Joe was screwing around so I jumped all over him. I was screaming at him and finally I threw him out of practice for being a pain in the ass. Yes, I threw my star guard out of the public practice on the eve of the Final Four.

After the practice I walked off the court all upset and a college coach stopped me and said, "Don, how do you talk to your black players that way?" I stopped in my tracks. I guess this guy had never seen a black player get hollered at, but I didn't even think about it. "The same way I talk to my white players," I said and kept moving. That probably should have told me just how big the race thing was going to be.

The most ironic thing about the entire 1966 season happened when we played Utah. Obviously, we went on to be the first team to start five black players in the national championship game and it broke the color barrier for a lot of teams in the South. But my black guys would never have gotten the chance to start in that game if it wasn't for one of their white teammates, Jerry Armstrong. We did a good job stopping that fast break but none of my big guys could stop Utah's Jerry Chambers. He wound up with thirty-eight points and seventeen rebounds and was fouling out every guy I sent out there to guard him. By the end, both Lattin and Harry Flournoy were out. Chambers was just unbelievable. Finally I put Armstrong on Chambers even though Armstrong had a sprained ankle. Well, he did better than anyone else had and slowed Chambers down at the end of the game. We won 85 to 78, but only because of Armstrong. Maybe Jerry Armstrong is the white guy who should get the credit for integrating college basketball. It sure as hell wasn't me guarding Jerry Chambers.

Kentucky beat Duke 83 to 79 in the other semifinal. Adolph Rupp was the coach, of course, and he had a hell of a team. They were called Rupp's Runts because they didn't have a starter over six foot five, but the guys they had were great. Pat Riley, Larry Conley, and Louis Dampier were all tremendously skilled players. They were an up-tempo team who loved to run, press, and shoot. Rupp was sixty-four years old then, had won over seven hundred games, and had won four national championships. He would go on to become the coach with the most wins in college basketball history until Dean Smith came along and broke Rupp's record. He was referred to as the Baron of the Bluegrass. When I was a freshman at Oklahoma A&M his team beat us for the national title. His Kentucky team that year included Ralph Beard, Lou Groza, and Wawa Jones. Our team was just a bunch of tough ole country boys from Oklahoma who could guard the hell out of you, but when it came to talent, we had very little. By 1966, Rupp was a larger-than-life figure to many in college basketball. A lot of people considered him the best coach in the country. I was thirty-six and born the same year Rupp started coaching. Five years before I had been a high school coach in a town in the panhandle of Texas that I doubt anyone in College Park, Maryland, had ever heard of. But I wasn't intimidated at all. I had played for Mr. Henry Iba, *the* greatest coach of all time. No coach intimidated me. None.

We had had a big press conference before the Final Four to hype up the event. There had to be at least one hundred people from the media there, more than I had ever seen. I remember Rupp getting up and sayin', "I been asked this a lot and I am willing to say that this year's team, if they win the tournament, is the best team that I've ever coached." I remember him saying that. It was a heck of a statement, but I wasn't bothered by it. He was telling the truth. I mean, they were a great offensive team. I think they were averaging ninety-some points a game. Rupp wasn't alone in his thinking. Most people thought Kentucky would beat us. The gamblers had installed them as a six-point favorite. Even though I respected Kentucky, mainly because they could really shoot the ball, I did not think it was the best team we would face that season. I thought Kansas was better. But I was loath to tell my players that. Even though everyone else considered us the underdog, my guys were already overconfident. They were just a loose, have-fun group playing without a lot of pressure. You play for a place such as Kentucky and you are supposed to win. You make the championship game at Texas Western and you truly have nothing to lose. So my players weren't nervous or tense.

Back at the hotel on the day of the final game I decided we needed to start three guards. Moe, my great friend Bill Cornwall, and I were in my room and I was telling them how good Kentucky's offense was and how we needed to move them off the wing position and pick up the ball when they tried to break. Again, at this point there was no scouting. We had no tapes. All I had on Kentucky was based on what Moe and I saw when they beat Duke in the semifinals. That was it. I also knew—or had been told—that Rupp's teams liked to run. This was the extent of our scouting information. The only good thing was they probably didn't have much more information on us, although it was possible considering the resources Kentucky had.

I knew we needed to get back on defense to stop the

break. That was fine, it was mostly the same thing we'd been doing all year, but in this case we couldn't afford any mistakes. Our guards had to dominate their guards and since they were the Runts we could afford to lose a big man. So I decided to start three guards. I also have to admit that I may have used race as a motivating factor. By this point the media was talking about it anyway and there was no way it hadn't entered my guys' thinking. Besides I was told Rupp had told some people privately that there was no way a black team would beat him. It got back to me that he was tellin' a joke, "What does TWC stand for? Two white coaches." I was a little pissed off about that. I didn't know if that was true, but during one of my meetings with the team on the afternoon of the day of the championship game, I mentioned to the players I had heard some rumors that Rupp had said that he "ain't losin' to a team of black players." I was trying to fire up their asses.

You want to know how much that worked, how concerned my guys were of the vaunted Kentucky Wildcats or supposedly playing for racial honors? A few hours later in the locker room before the game I was laying out the plan, putting something on the blackboard. I looked over and Bobby Joe was lying over in the corner asleep. He had a toothpick stuck right here in the middle of his mouth, propping it open. He was taking a damn Sunday nap just before the national championship game. I grabbed an eraser and beaned him with it. If I'd had something heavier to throw I would have thrown that, I was so angry I couldn't think straight. The eraser woke him up and sent chalk flying all over the locker room. And I screamed, I said, "I hope you get your ass kicked. I am so damn sick and tired of this crap!"

With that I just left the locker room. Moe and I went and got a cup of coffee, and I said, "Moe, let's just get our asses beat tonight and get outta here. Screw these guys. Let them get embarrassed on national television." It was funny because as the story goes now, the Kentucky players say they saw intensity in our eyes. Intensity? My ass. My guys were taking naps, daydreaming, looking for girls in the stands. This was the loosest team I ever had. By that point even I was no longer tight. You get used to it. I mean, you see it and say, "Well, there we go. Nothin' I can do about it anyway."

Because of my decision to go with three guards, my starting five that night was a new lineup. Bobby Joe Hill, Orsten Artis, David Lattin, and Harry Flournoy were regular starters most of the year. But tonight five-foot-six Willie Worsley was going to start in place of Nevil Shed and be the third guard. I almost started Willie Cager because Flournoy had hurt his knee against Utah, but Flournoy said he could go. I just wasn't sure for how long. My theory was Kentucky could beat us only if we let them run. Worsley was so fast that he would help us get back to stop the break. Normally when we shot the ball we would have two guys get back on defense and three try to get an offensive rebound. That night we decided we'd send two to the boards—Flournoy (and shortly Cager) and Lattin (or Shed when he was in)—and send three back— Hill, Worsley, and Artis. Kentucky loved to get the defensive rebound, look for the outlet pass, and push the ball up the court. But with three guys committed to defending the break, we snuffed out most of their fast-break opportunities. It is very difficult to get anything going when three guys that good at "on the ball" defense are waiting for you.

Three guards also let us walk it up. I wanted to control the tempo of the game, get it played in the 70s and not the 90s. I knew that Kentucky liked to trap defensively, but I wasn't sure how. So going in I thought we needed that extra guard and it turned out to be true. Nothing gets a fast break offense going like defensive turnovers. It gives the other team easy baskets. We just couldn't allow that if we wanted to win.

When the game started there was no noticeable reaction from the players or the fans about the racial aspect of the game. None. It was just another game. It may have gone down in history, but at the time I don't think anyone even considered it. Once the game started Kentucky jumped into Rupp's traditional 1–3–1 zone, which Rupp called a trap, to create turnovers. I had never seen it before. I wasn't even sure what kind of defense they were playing at first. So I told Hill to take a time-out and then I told them to "pass the ball around for a minute, let's practice against this thing, see how it works, how it reacts to different things and then figure out how to beat it." I could do that because my players were such smart players. They drove me nuts, but you could never argue with their basketball IQ. So we get out there, pass it around, go into the post, and out for about forty-five seconds (remember, there was no shot clock back then). After the zone exposed itself I called time-out, got out a piece of paper, and said, "It's a one-three-one zone; this is how we beat it."

Hill and Worsley were such great ball handlers that they wouldn't be bothered much by a trapping zone. They took care of the ball, and if one got trapped he could always pass to another equally gifted dribbler. A full-court trap works in college because usually the other team doesn't have more than one really good ball handler. In the NBA just about everyone can handle it, which is the reason you don't see full-court presses much in the pros. Kentucky broke us a couple times, but not much. Three point guards enabled us to beat the trap and slow the game way, way down. Once the tempo was where I wanted it, I would slip another big guy in there. But mainly we played with three guards.

We conceded some rebounding, but I thought Lattin would be able to hold his own, due in part to intimidation. I knew a lot was being made of the white-black thing and although I didn't care about it I wasn't going to ignore it. I knew that the Kentucky guys had surely never seen a player as physically intimidating as David Lattin so they might be susceptible to being intimidated by him. Hell, Lattin could intimidate anyone of any race. So I told Lattin that on our first possession we were going to float it to the baseline and get him the ball. I said, "David, I want you to take it to the rim and dunk it on someone. Just knock them over. Just dunk it like they ain't never seen it dunked. Not in person, not on television. I don't care if you get called for a charge, for traveling, rip off the backboard, anything. Just dunk the damn thing. Take it at their center and run his ass over."

This was a bit of coaching that Lattin followed to a T. The game started and sure enough, we got the ball to Lattin

and he headed to the rim. Damn, their center saw him coming and just ran. Just ran his ass out of there. You could hardly
blame him. To see the two-hundred-forty-pound David Lattin charging down the lane was one scary sight. Only one guy
tried to defend the play, Pat Riley. I respected him for that.
These days you see him with his hair slicked back and all
those fancy suits, but he was a street-tough Schenectady, New
York, boy. But tough or not, he wasn't two hundred forty
pounds like David. Of course, David dunked it on his head,
just slammed it right down on his head. No foul. No travel.
Just two points for the Miners. After that, I felt we had the intimidation factor. It didn't hurt that a couple plays later Riley
tried to take it to the rim on us and David not only blocked
his attempt to jam it in, but slammed Riley to the floor as
well. Lattin just owned the middle and it wasn't by playing
dirty. I've said this many times after the game was over, every
one of the Kentucky players came down and shook his hand.
They respected him.

Oddly enough the most memorable thing about the actual game was the lack of memorable moments. For the most
part it was a good, clean, hard-fought game between two very
good teams. The two big plays came courtesy of Bobby Joe,
who may have been napping before the game, but made big
plays during it. I had told Bobby Joe before the game that
Louis Dampier was a great ball handler and not to mess
around too much trying to steal the ball. Just play good defense. Shed hit a free throw to give us a 10 to 9 lead with
10:18 left in the first half. Dampier, covered by Bobby Joe,

brought the ball up for Kentucky and one-on-one at half court Bobby Joe stole it from him and drove it in for a layup. All of a sudden it was 12 to 9 with 10:06 remaining. Dampier regrouped and started bringing the ball up again, this time more cautiously. But Bobby Joe was just so quick that right at center court he did it again, picking Dampier's pocket and going in for another layup, 14 to 9 us with 9:56 to go. A couple minutes later he made a circus scoop-shot layup that dazzled the crowd.

Bobby Joe did more than give us a five-point lead with those plays. I think he shocked Kentucky. Everyone in Cole Fieldhouse must have thought that anytime Bobby Joe wanted to steal that ball from Louis Dampier he could. Bobby Joe certainly thought that. He came over to the bench later and asked me, "How many times do you want me to steal it?" It was a backbreaking sequence and on top of what Lattin was doing I believe we really rattled the Wildcats. "Hill hurt us— hurt us real bad with those two steals in the first half," Rupp told the media after. Until then I wasn't sure how much they respected us. After the game Rupp said, "We came here to beat Duke and might have keyed too much on them." And maybe his players sensed that. I don't know. Supposedly Rupp was furious at halftime, a *Sports Illustrated* reporter who was in their locker room quoted him as saying he didn't want to lose to a bunch of "coons." Whatever he said, we didn't know about it at the time. Moe and I were just trying to keep the guys concentrating on winning the game. We were twenty minutes from a national title.

I have to give the Kentucky players credit, they never quit. They couldn't run like they were used to and get easy baskets. In fact, they could hardly run at all. I have to credit that Utah defensive drill again. We were just so prepared to handle fast-break teams. Looking back through the old newspaper clippings from that game I discovered a photo in the *El Paso Times*. It shows three Kentucky players—Tommy Kron, Larry Conley, and Thad Jaracz—trying to get a fast break going and David Lattin jamming the three of them up all by himself. Our center is somehow guarding three players in transition all at once. You learn to do that when you play two-on-five. My guys were guarding them tightly, jersey to jersey, number to number. Kentucky was one of the best shooting teams I had ever seen, but they went just twenty-seven for seventy (38.5 percent) for the game. Both Dampier and Riley had nineteen points, but they shot a combined fifteen for forty to get it.

We were patient and efficient. We completely controlled the pace of the game. We shot twenty-two of forty-nine (44.9 percent) and beat them by two (thirty-five to thirty-three) on the boards. Bobby Joe had twenty points, Lattin had sixteen and nine rebounds. Bobby Joe's two steals gave us a lead we never relinquished. UK got the score down to one point a couple of times, but our guys never rattled. Hill kept making clutch shots to get us going again. By the end they never really threatened us. We led by eleven with 3:22 remaining. It didn't end up a blowout, but we won fairly easily, 72 to 65.

After the game I told the media it was our ability to guard them that led to the victory. "It was the defense," I said. "It seemed like we've been able to do it like that all season when we had to. Before the game we feared their shooting. It was the best offensive team we played, but our team defense was excellent. We've kept teams to lower scores, but we weren't playing teams that had such good shooters." Rupp agreed. Sort of. He said a flu bug had been going through the team, which may have affected things. He added that his kids didn't play well when they were considered the overwhelming favorites. "The pressure got to us a little. Our boys did things they shouldn't. Our offense was not challenging their defense."

I didn't pay much attention to what Rupp was saying then—although I would later. I was pleased to have won the title, although not as excited as you would think. Mainly I was just happy the season was over. The championship game was more of a relief than something to celebrate. I didn't have to fight these guys anymore. It was a draining season down to the last straw. I had to be the least excited championship coach of all time. My players were excited, but it wasn't a big party or anything, not one of those champagne locker room celebrations you see on television these days. They were a laid-back team. I know my three New York players (Shed, Worsley, and Cager) were excited because back then the NCAA championship team usually got invited to appear on *The Ed Sullivan Show*, which was filmed in Manhattan. So they were more excited about a free trip back home to New York than winning the championship. Of course, in a sign of things to come, Ed Sullivan didn't invite Texas Western to appear on his show.

When we tried to land at El Paso we couldn't because so many fans had come out on the tarmac to welcome us home (this was before the days of ramps) that they were actually crowding the runway. We had nowhere to land. So we circled the airport once or twice to get the runway cleared and then finally landed.

Police estimated at the time that there was a crowd of ten thousand people waiting for us. I believe it. It took us forever to get off the plane, walk to where our bags were, get on the bus, and so on. It was a mob scene. When the bus finally got going, a parade followed us all the way from the airport to downtown, with solid people the whole way. That is a long way, over ten miles.

I was tired, but it was wonderful to see the people of El Paso so excited. In six short seasons I had grown to love the city and the school, so it meant a lot to me to give the people something to be proud of. And it was one of the reasons why, when some bigger, richer schools came a-calling after I had led little Texas Western to the national title, I never left. El Paso was my home now.

THIRTEEN

THE FALLOUT

Two things Haskins isn't much for are honors and crowds. One of his most vivid memories of his 1997 enshrinement into the Naismith Hall of Fame is that he had to wear a tuxedo and give a speech. He's a simple guy. Which is why I was surprised in 2000 when he called and told me he was not just coming to the Final Four that year in Minneapolis, but he was staying a night. This was un-Haskins-like.

    He wouldn't tell me why though. He just said to meet him at a certain address at 7:00 P.M. and "We'll get a beer." When Haskins says "we'll get a beer," it means you are not going to get "a beer." You are going to have more than "a beer" and that is before the tequila gets involved. And you certainly aren't going to any fern-filled martini bar; he'd rather eat a salad than darken the door of one of those places. It is going to be dim, smoky, full of character and characters, and if there is food, it is coming from the Fry-O-Later.

These are my kind of places, so I was more than up for it. But needless to say, you don't dress up for a night like that. T-shirt, jeans, maybe some work boots. Come as you are since you sure as hell aren't trying to impress anyone.

The problem was, the address he gave me turned out to be a giant, brightly lit theater, with hundreds of NCAA high rollers arriving in smart suits and nice dresses. It turns out we were meeting at the official NCAA Final Four kickoff function. Haskins, no matter how much he wished it wasn't so, was going to receive a lifetime achievement award from the NCAA.

CBS's Jim Nantz was the master of ceremonies. Everyone from the president of the NCAA to every influential athletic director to each of the Final Four coaches was in the house. So too were a bunch of television executives and editors from the elite national sports magazines and newspapers.

This was the place to be for the upwardly mobile, which is the kind of game I've never been very good at playing. Not that I was used to losing this bad. Everyone else was in his Sunday best. I looked ready to change my oil. Whatever remotely slim chance there was of continuing my career with some fancy media organization, I supposed it was pretty much over at that point.

A minute later Haskins arrived looking sharp by his

standards—which meant his plaid button-down shirt had no
barbeque stains on it.

We wound up sitting in the front row—no place to hide with
five hundred sets of eyes on us. Nantz gave him a wonderful
introduction and called him up on stage to interview him. Everyone
applauded.

For just about anyone else in college athletics this would have
been a big deal, a big night, a chance to soak up some well-earned
praise. Make no mistake, Haskins was appreciative and polite. He is
a gentleman at heart.

But this was the media and NCAA power base that had made
life miserable for him, his players, and his program after he dared
start five black players all those years ago. The old cowboy had
neither forgotten nor forgiven, so he didn't let the opportunity pass
without getting some shots in.

He noted his decision was quite unpopular at the time. He
named some names in the media. He went on to criticize the
NCAA for not selecting his team (as well as others from the West)
to the tournament more often—"Y'all are obsessed with the Big
East." Then got after them for the confusing and corrupt way it
enforces its myriad rules since, he noted, it is generally the big schools
that are cheating their asses off, but the small ones who get
punished.

The audience didn't quite know how to react. It was classic, one
of the truly great acceptance speeches of all time and pure give 'em
hell Bear Haskins. He did everything but tell them he was late for a
date with a bottle of tequila, which may have caused a mass
fainting.

"You screwed me," I laughed later, not a bit upset, once we had found that dark bar, a longneck, and a shot of El Señor sitting in front of us. "Why didn't you tell me we were going to an awards ceremony? I would have worn a suit."

He shrugged his shoulders.

"You always need someone to be dressed worse than you are. That way, when they are talkin' about the guy who doesn't know how to dress right, they ain't talking about you."

Just like so many unsuspecting snooker opponents through the years, the old hustler had hustled me bad.

I bought the next round. It was an honor.

■

I've said this many times over the last forty years, but for a long time I thought winning the national championship was the worst thing ever to happen to me. I wished for a long time that we had never won that game with Kentucky because life would have been a heck of a lot easier for me, my school, and my players.

That is not a sentiment shared by everyone. Since 1966 a lot of people have come up to me and thanked me. Hell, you'd think it happened yesterday. In El Paso it is an everyday occurrence. People are grateful here for that title. They stop me in restaurants, grocery stores, wherever. I haven't coached since 1999 and the people still want pictures, autographs. I understand that and am humbled. I guess it is to be expected in El Paso. I should have anticipated that when we won the title.

But it isn't just here or in west Texas. It is everywhere. No matter where I travel people come up and thank me for starting five black players. I'd be somewhere, decades later, and all of a sudden a black man would come up to me and want to shake my hand and thank me because after the 1966 game, schools throughout the country began integrating and he got a scholarship somewhere because of it. One I appreciated the most was from Chuck Foreman, the great NFL running back. I was at the airport in Phoenix and he stopped me and he said, "I've always wanted to thank you for giving black guys like myself a chance to go to school." He just said all the right things, and it made me feel real good.

This kind of stuff would just blow my mind. It was incredible. All I ever sought out to do was win the game. I certainly did not expect to be some racial pioneer or change the world. Nolan Richardson would declare I was responsible for "thousands of scholarships for blacks in the South." I just couldn't see it that way at the time. Race was the farthest thing from my mind.

But the game did have an impact, I must admit. Within a week of winning the national championship the hate mail flowed in by the garbage bucket. I had received hate mail before because we had black players, but not like this. There were bags and bags of nasty, racist, ignorant letters. Most of them came from the South and a lot of them from Kentucky.

Our campus postman couldn't even handle them all. Eventually the school estimated I received forty thousand pieces of mail. I sure as hell didn't read them all. It took only a few for me to know what they all said.

Every one of them was just disgusting to me. These were just college kids playing basketball. What did anyone care? We were just this little ole school in dusty west Texas that no one had ever heard of and now people all over the country hated us because we had black student-athletes. It was almost too much to fathom.

The positive impact of the game came through increased opportunity for black players. Before we beat Kentucky there was not a single black basketball or football player in the Southeastern, Southwest, or Atlantic Coast Conference. Not one. A couple months after we won, Vanderbilt of the SEC recruited the first black basketball player and the floodgates opened. I remember looking at the sports page in the early 1970s and they had pictures of the members of the All-Southwest Conference team. All five of them were black. It was that quick. Within five, six years everyone was recruiting black players because if they didn't they wouldn't be able to field a competitive team. Heck, even Adolph Rupp eventually recruited a black player.

But not before Adolph Rupp said some things to anger me. He couldn't deal with losing, and he took it out on my players. He said at some coaching clinics my players were "a bunch of crooks." He said my guys weren't real students. He told the *Courier-Journal* of Louisville that I had recruited David

Lattin out of Tennessee State *Prison*, when in fact David had been a student at Tennessee State *University*. I know this sounds impossible now for stories like that to get printed, but you have to consider the times.

In Kentucky the papers would print just anything. Facts meant nothing. It was incredible. I remember reading that in 2004 the *Lexington Herald-Leader* wrote an apology to its readers for purposely not writing about the civil rights movement in the 1960s. The paper said it was trying to keep the status quo and keep local blacks from joining the protests for equal rights. So if there were a big event the paper would just ignore it, pretend it didn't happen. According to the newspaper, there were no riots, no marches. It decided what the news was and that was that. So when Rupp would say stuff, the Kentucky papers would print it. No need to check facts. According to them, there wasn't even a civil rights movement.

Normally I wouldn't care what they were saying about me in Kentucky, but in college sports, recruiting is everything. If you don't have players you can't win. It was Bobby Joe making those steals in the championship game, not me. So when something negative gets printed in the paper you can bet every coach in the country recruiting against me is going to get his hands on it and send it to the recruit, his coach, his parents, whomever.

It was just beginning after the Final Four when Rupp and I were named co-national coaches of the year by the Knights of Columbus. They had a big convention in Columbus, Ohio, and at the time this was a big deal. If I had known then everything Rupp was saying about me I would have confronted him, but at this point he was just starting. We were both there for the ceremony. I shook hands with him and he glared at me. Rupp spoke first and after he was done I spoke and I made a point to talk about some of the great teams we played that year. I mentioned how great Cincinnati was. And how great Utah was. And how great Kansas and Oklahoma City were. But I never mentioned Kentucky. I never said a single word about Kentucky. I was tryin' to stick a needle in his ass and don't think for a second he didn't know it.

After that things got tough. *Sports Illustrated* came to town after we won the title and did a story on black athletes at TWC that, incredibly, said I exploited black players; that our kids weren't real students and El Paso was a community that was unfriendly to minorities. I hit the roof. The magazine was so irresponsible I couldn't believe it. In one part of the story it suggested that El Paso was so racist that none of my players' wives could get jobs there. Wives? None of my players were even married. I used to respect that magazine, but like a lot of people who have dealt with it through the years, I realized its purpose isn't about telling the truth. It just writes what it wants to write. Its goal is to create controversy.

We tried to get our athletic director, George McCarty, to file a lawsuit against *Sports Illustrated,* but he wouldn't do it. He thought it would be better just to let it blow over. I deeply, deeply regret that I didn't file one myself, but I thought that the additional attention was unfair to my players, my school, and my city. This was a mistake and perhaps the biggest regret of my life. I have never forgiven the magazine. Not to this very day. That magazine hurt my players and their parents. And it was wrong. Then, to add insult to injury, several years later in 1976 James Michener released a book called *Sports in America*. Michener didn't do any new research, he just repeated all of the falsehoods that were in *Sports Illustrated*. In fact, he admitted as much when confronted by two English professors at the university here, Mimi Gladstein and Les Standiford, that he had relied entirely on Jack Olsen's article in *Sports Illustrated*.

Michener referred to our championship as "one of the most wretched episodes in the history of American sport." Can you believe that? We were just college kids playing basketball. How can that be wretched? He claimed my players were criminals and nonstudents. I just couldn't believe this stuff. I was sick over it. I remember at the time talking to one of my former players, Steve Tredennick, a practicing lawyer in El Paso, about suing Michener—not for the money though. I just wanted to get him into an El Paso courtroom so I might get close enough to get my hands around his neck, haul his ass outside, and drag him through the weeds for a while. A good ass-kicking might have been satisfaction enough for me. It may not have been, but I certainly wished I had tested out that theory. I deeply, deeply regret to this day I didn't.

This is what happens though, when you upset the apple-cart. Kentucky was a nationally established power. All-white teams such as Duke, Maryland, North Carolina, and Texas had a lot of power. They were the establishment and our little commuter school screwed everything up. There were plenty of whites at those schools that didn't want to see blacks on the team, blacks in college. But now if they didn't integrate their teams would never be able to remain competitive. So the establishment struck back by trying to crush us, humiliate us, ruin us. And in a lot of ways they did it. I had no way to fight back. Our local papers at the time, the *El Paso Times* and the *El Paso Herald-Post*, didn't exactly go national. To this day it still makes me sick to think what the media did to the reputations of these fine young men. My players had done nothing wrong but attend college and play basketball. They could say what they wanted about me, but not my players.

It wasn't long before I was receiving a new version of hate mail. No longer was it ignorant whites calling me a "nigger lover," it was black ministers calling me an exploiter. All of a sudden *I* was the racist. Supposedly I was just using black kids to win games and I didn't care at all about them. I remember Nolan Richardson was in town one day in the late 1960s and I showed him the letters and I said, "Nolan, can you believe this crap?" And he read them, just shook his head, and said, "Coach, we've got them on both sides."

Anyone who tells you that our 1966 team was celebrated across the country for what we accomplished is lying. We were loved in El Paso. And certainly there were blacks who saw us on television and couldn't believe their eyes and loved what we did. But the establishment and the media it controls was completely against us. We were pariahs. We were villains. We were the "wretched." We were not being held up as heroes. If you had told me then that one day Walt Disney Studios would make a major motion picture honoring that team, I would have thought you were plumb crazy. If you told me I would one day be writing a book released by Hyperion Books, a major publishing house in New York City, I would have laughed at you. There was just no way. None.

After all of the fallout, recruiting was virtually impossible. Instead of using the championship to attract more good players, we had to fight all the negative press. Opposing coaches would for years travel around with a copy of that *Sports Illustrated* story in their briefcases. They'd go to a home visit with someone we were recruiting and pull it out.

For the record I want to state what each of my players on the 1966 national championship team went on to do and you can decide whether they were real students or exploited:

- David Lattin, public relations executive, Houston, Texas

- Bobby Joe Hill, retired executive, El Paso Natural Gas Co., El Paso, Texas. Died in 2002.

- Harry Flournoy, route sales representative, Bimbo Bakeries USA, El Segundo, California

- Dick Myers, vice president planning and logistics, Coach Leather, Inc., New York City

- Nevil Shed, coordinator of student programs for the University Center, University of Texas, San Antonio, Texas

- Willie Worsley, dean of students (retired), Boys Choir of Harlem, New York City, and currently head basketball coach at Spring Valley High School, Spring Valley, New York

- Orsten Artis, lead detective (retired), Gary, Indiana, police department

- Willie Cager, teacher and high school basketball coach (retired), Tornillo, Texas

- Jerry Armstrong, teacher and basketball coach (retired), at multiple high schools in Missouri

- Togo Railey, dual master's degrees, ex-basketball coach, assistant principal (retired), Port Neches-Groves, Texas

- Louis Baudoin, master's degree in education, high school teacher and coach (retired), Albuquerque, New Mexico

- David Palacio, executive vice president/CFO Univision Music, Los Angeles

There were more negatives also. First off, opposing fans would get all over us. They do that no matter who you are playing, that's fans bein' fans, but it takes on a different emotion when race is involved. I knew it wouldn't be easy for some of my guys not to react. This is tough both for black guys and white guys. The black guys for obvious reasons. But the white guys because they want to defend their teammates. My players never had racial problems. So I had a rule. I told the team,

"You know, they call me some damn names too. You think I don't hear all that crap?" So my rule was if they ever saw me turn around even one time and acknowledge some fan, if I let on that they're gettin' to me, then they can do it too. They could do whatever. But if I don't ever do it, if I don't ever turn around, then by God they better not do it either. That kept them in check and kept me in check, because there were some necks I wanted to wring, I'll tell you that. But I knew if I did, half my team would be in the stands slugging fans and that would be that. It was a good rule.

Unfortunately it went beyond heckling though. During the 1966–67 season we were set to play a game in Dallas against Southern Methodist. The afternoon of the game I was in my hotel room working on the game plan and there was this crazy knock at my door. I answered it and Nevil Shed comes barging in, all hyped up. He said, "Coach, Coach, some cat just called me and said if I take the floor [against SMU] he is going to shoot my black ass." I told Shed to calm down, he was always a little excitable so I didn't know what to believe. But pretty soon my phone rings and sure enough here is some redneck saying, "You mother so-and-so, if you play all those niggers you're going to get your ass shot." I told him a few things and called him a few names back before he hung up. The same guy called Willie Cager and a few other players too.

I never told the newspapers about it and I didn't even want to take it seriously, but this was an era when people were getting assassinated. You couldn't ignore it. In 1963 right there in Dallas someone shot President Kennedy. I figured if they

could kill the president of the United States they could probably kill some ole basketball coach or one of his players pretty
easily. A year later, in 1968, both Dr. Martin Luther King and
Bobby Kennedy would be killed. There were all sorts of
killings associated with the civil rights movement and unwit-
tingly, just by coaching college basketball, I guess I had somehow put myself into the middle of it. That was the reality of
the time, so I called the FBI and told them about the calls.

That night I could barely get out of our locker room
there were so many FBI guys in the hallway. I appreciated it
but I was getting fed up too. I sure as hell didn't want to lose
the game and everyone was on edge. We took the floor and
you couldn't help but look up in the stands. In a way it was
kind of funny. We were in the pregame huddle and Shed is
running around the thing. He wouldn't lean in and listen, he
was just running little laps around the huddle. I finally yell,
"Shed, what the hell are you doing?" And Shed being Shed
says, "Coach, if someone is going to take a shot at me, I'm at
least going to be a moving target."

Well, it turned out the phone calls were thankfully just
threats and nothing happened. I don't know, maybe it was all
the FBI guys. We even won the game, 71 to 62, and I'll tell
you, I never got my team off the floor quicker. Usually when
players win a game they like to stay on the floor for a minute
or two and enjoy it, maybe shake hands with the other team.
Not that night, we were in the locker room in about five seconds, sportsmanship be damned. I have never been happier to
be done with a game.

Most coaches are just like me, we want to win. To win you need to have the best players and that means recruiting from the broadest possible talent pool. If you discriminate you are freezing out potential players. It is that simple. So it wasn't long after 1966 that a lot of coaches who had previously only dealt with whites found themselves with black players. Not all of them adjusted as quickly as I did.

Back then one of the schools of thought was that blacks were great athletes but they weren't smart players. You could use them as rebounders but not as point guards. It was the same in football when for years blacks weren't supposed to be smart enough to play quarterback. Remember that? Blacks were running backs, receivers, and linebackers, but until 1988 when Doug Williams came along and led the Washington Redskins to victory in Super Bowl XXII they weren't quarterbacks. Now the NFL is full of black quarterbacks who look damn smart enough to me—Donovan McNabb, Steve McNair, Michael Vick. It is almost incredible that anyone ever thought that way.

Well, that was also what they said about point guards. But that never entered my mind. Hell, Bobby Joe was one smart player, a genius on the court in many ways. I think a lot of my beliefs went back to playing with Herman Carr. Like I told you, he was a smart player. He knew the game better than I did for a long time. I learned from him. So it never crossed my mind that a guy who was black could never run a team. I always believed anyone could do it as long as he was disciplined and disciplining him was my job. That was the key;

you had to discipline your point guard, no matter what race he was. He had to be the coach on the floor, the most disciplined player out there. So you couldn't consider race when doing that. If he was black, like Bobby Joe Hill, you had to ride his ass until he learned what to do. You couldn't just discipline the white guys.

After 1966 this was a lesson a lot of coaches were just learning. I'll never forget in 1971 when we played in the Sun Carnival tournament in El Paso. Florida State, Southern California, and Miami of Ohio were in the field. Hugh Durham was the coach at Florida State and he had three or four black players all of a sudden. They had a black guy who wore a sweatband around his head. They played Southern Cal in the first round and they were going down the damn floor and I guess the sweatband player was upset at something so he goes and sits down on the bench. He just takes himself out of the game in the middle of the action. Now they are out there playing with four. Of course they get scored on and then Hugh calls time-out and gets a sub in there. Not surprisingly USC won the game to meet us in the championship game the next night.

Southern Cal had Paul Westphal then and it was a great team. The Trojans went 24 and 2 that season and only UCLA's dominance kept them from winning the national championship. Their only two losses that season were to the Bruins, so Los Angeles had the two best teams in the country. But when we got down to them in the first half I wasn't taking any solace in that. I was so pissed off I could hardly stand it. I got into that locker room and went nuts. I was screaming at this player and hollering at that player, saying this, saying that. I was tough on those guys. I didn't care who was who and certainly didn't care what their skin color was. I was trying to wake them up before we got our asses beat (we wound up making a great game of it before losing 65 to 63). Anyway, at the end of the tirade, I turned and as I stormed out of the locker room I kicked the door open.

Well, as the door swung open it slammed into Hugh Durham, almost knocking him down. He was playing Miami of Ohio in the consolation game, but I guess he had been walking by the locker room door and overheard my halftime fit. I felt bad I hit Hugh with the door, but I was so angry at my team it didn't really sink in. Hugh regrouped, looked at me, and said with a bit of wonder, "How can you talk to black players like that?" And it shocked me. I said, "What the hell do you talk to them about? These guys weren't playing defense, why should I care if they are black." And he said, "You can't talk to black players like that." And I said, "Well, why shouldn't I?" Then I just walked away. But it was interesting and telling that he would think like that. That was what his problem was at that time. He was not being tough enough on his black players and the team was falling apart due to lack of cohesiveness, chemistry, and discipline. You can't win that way, even if you think at the time it is best to baby some players.

Now, in all fairness, I want to say Hugh was a really good coach. And he sorted it all out pretty quickly, by the way. The next season Florida State went to the 1972 Final Four. You can't do that unless everyone is playing together. I think he was yelling at everybody equally by then. And I sincerely doubt any of the black players on that team felt like shaking my hand for giving them an opportunity while it was happening. But it was all part of the changing landscape of college basketball, something we had inadvertently caused in 1966.

FOURTEEN

RECRUITING BATTLES

"We were recruiting Greg Foster out of Oakland, California, one year," Haskins said as we sat around nursing a couple of Buds in a near empty Rosa's Cantina, the somewhat famous beer bar down near the river on the west side of El Paso. "And Greg tells us about this guard in town who he says is good. I said, 'Who's after him?' And Greg said, 'Well, nobody, but they're wrong. This guard is really something else.'

"So I decide to look into it, mainly to appease Greg. And heck, the kid might be able to play a little. Players do know other players. So I felt the least I can do is bring him to El Paso for a visit. When *he got to campus I had him play some pickup ball with my current players. The NCAA doesn't let coaches watch, so afterwards I asked some of my guards how he was. And they said, 'Aw, he's OK.' Well, you can't take a word that those guys say seriously, you have to translate it. Those are my current players who are looking for playing time. The last thing they want me to do is bring in a great player in their position that might affect that.*

"So now I'm thinking, If he was real bad, they would tell me, 'Aw, coach, he's great.' They would want me to sign him because they know they can beat him out. If they say he is terrible, then he is probably really good. Based on the lukewarm evaluation of my current players, I figured he was pretty good and I liked his personality, so I offered him a scholarship. I wanted him to take it right then and there because I admit, I wasn't one of those coaches who loved recruiting. I was fixin' to play golf so I just wanted to get some guys signed and get recruitin' over.

"Well, the kid says he can't sign right then because he promised to visit St. John's. He wouldn't break his promise. He said, 'Coach I want to come. I'll sign next week.' Right at the same time we had found a kid in Baton Rouge, Louisiana, who wasn't half bad. So I told both players, first one to commit gets the scholarship. The kid from Baton Rouge jumps on it. Fine, I go and play golf.

"But every morning I come into the office for a few minutes before going to the golf course and there is a message from the guard from Oakland. He didn't get offered a scholarship by St. John's so he is calling, begging me to take him, call him, anything. Just give him a chance. I was out of scholarships at this point though. One morning I am in there and my secretary, Diana Lubianski, says the

kid is on the phone. So I decide that enough is enough, I need to be blunt and end this. So I picked up the phone and said . . .

"Now Gary Payton, I just can't take you."

■

You never, ever know in recruiting. Which is why it can drive you crazy. The guy who you think is going to be an all-star turns out to be a dog. A kid you won't take a phone call from becomes Gary Payton, NBA All-Star. Years later I asked St. John's coach Lou Carnesecca about Payton. I said, "What the hell didn't you like about him?" And Lou said, "I was about half-loaded." He was joking, of course, but he said, "Can you believe we blew that one?" And both of us are in the Hall of Fame. But that's recruiting. You just never know.

Still, a coach is nothing without players, which is why recruiting is such an important part of college basketball. And I learned a lot about recruiting in the summer of 1972 when I was an assistant coach on the U.S. Olympic team. Mr. Iba was the head coach in 1972, his third time heading up the Olympic team. He asked me to be an assistant and of course I jumped at the chance. Back then the Olympic teams were made of true college all-stars. There were just twelve slots and we had tryouts in Colorado Springs. Just about every great college player tried out for the team. One of my own players, Jim Forbes, made the team.

One day during the Olympics in Munich, Germany, we

were in the hotel elevator. It was me, Jim, and about three or four players. Out of nowhere one of them asks Jim, "What kind of car you got?" Jim looked down and was embarrassed. He said, "Aw, I don't have a car." Since I'm on the elevator all of the other guys look at me. One says to me, "Are you tellin' me you got a player this good and he doesn't have a car? Do any of your players have a car?" They didn't mean *have* a car. They could have a car if they bought it themselves. They meant, had I *bought* them a car. And I said, "No, I haven't bought any damn cars." The players sort of laughed, but it really pissed me off. And I guess Jim found out that everybody that could play a little bit had a car. I had no idea. I knew a lot of schools did that, but I didn't think they all did. Well, I was wrong.

It was funny though. Since Mr. Iba was getting up in years—he had retired from Oklahoma A&M in 1971 and this was the summer of 1972—I had to be the badass coach, the one who would give the players hell. Before the Olympics we were practicing three times a day and tryin' to catch up with the other national teams that had been together twelve years. We were runnin' defensive drills and it was hard on 'em. I didn't give an inch. We really got that team together. One of those players in the elevator had never had anyone say anything to him. I think he was surprised coaches talked that way to players. But he also took to it and really improved.

The next year that player's team came to El Paso to play us and they had the damnedest team you've ever seen. They had a six-foot-nine guard with a gold tooth who was somethin' else. The guy got my home number and called me. I liked him so I met him for a cup of coffee here in town. He asked me if I would go speak to his coach. I was like, "Why?" And he said, "We've got to have discipline. We could have a hell of a team if we had discipline. You know, with our school, you don't have to go to practice if you don't want to."

I kind of laughed and I said, "I'll tell you what. Take your damned car back and maybe your coach might discipline you. How in the hell can he discipline you if he's given you something?" Well, he didn't deny he had gotten some stuff, but he didn't think that should make any difference. But it does. And that always stuck with me. Here's an ole boy begging for discipline who can't get it because he's been corrupted. You just can't coach players you have paid. At least I never thought you could.

But that sure cost me some recruits. I don't think people even understand how widespread cheating is.

Some guys would cheat and they'd drive me crazy. Other guys I liked anyway. I remember being up in Wisconsin where I spent some time at a summer camp with Al McGuire, who coached Marquette in the 1970s and went on to be a famous broadcaster. He passed away a couple years back. Al was a real character from New York, one of the funniest guys you'd ever meet. We went fishin' and did all this and that. We became friends. We are talking one night and Al says, "Now, Don, I really like ya. You're a good guy. So let me tell you this and I want you to trust me. If we're ever recruiting a guy that you're recruiting, and I tell you I want him, don't screw with him. Don't waste your time. Because I'll get him. I'm gonna get him." And I believed him. That was Al. He didn't just say stuff.

A few years later we were recruiting a kid from just outside of Chicago. He was a really good player and I wanted him so we spent a lot of time on him and called him all the time. Then one day Al calls me and says, "Hey, Don, I'm going after this guy and I'm going to get him." Well, I think we are in there pretty good, the player has given me all the reason in the world to think that he might be coming to UTEP, so I don't listen. I thought maybe Al knows how well-positioned we are and is just trying to scare me away. I go back to Chicago and have a helluva visit with this kid's mom and dad. I'm feeling real good as I'm going out the door when damn if this car doesn't pull up and out pops Al McGuire, tie on, carrying a briefcase. I don't know what he had in his briefcase, but it was a little suspicious. When he saw me he stopped just dead still. He was shocked and said, "Don, what the hell you doin' here?" And I said, "Recruitin'. I'm recruitin' this guy." He shook his head like he couldn't believe what kind of a fool I was and said, "Now, Don, I told you as a friend not to waste your time with guys I'm recruiting." I didn't know what to say. All I know is the next time I called that player, who had always been so eager to speak to me, he wasn't available. The next time I called him he wasn't available. I never spoke to the kid on the phone again. He went to Marquette. At least ole Al wasn't lying to me.

One thing I didn't do much of in recruiting was watch kids play high school games. I don't think in all of my coaching I missed one day of practice for recruiting. I never believed that a coach ought to take off and not take care of the guys he's already got. I was always more interested in getting the guys I had to be better, not just getting new players. Maybe I'd go see a kid in El Paso, or if we were on a road trip and had a free night, in Houston or Denver. But even that was rare. Coaches nowadays are never around their teams. Recruiting is important but I think that takes away from actual coaching.

This wasn't the only thing that put me behind the eight-ball during my coaching career. I was stubborn in the face of a lot of new ways of recruiting. There was a time I wouldn't sign a kid with a tattoo—try that these days. I was opposed to just about anything that pampered the players, even if most schools were engaging in just that kind of stuff. I just didn't see how making life easy for a kid helped make him a better basketball player. Mr. Iba never made things easy for us, so why should I make it easy for my players?

Tim Floyd came to work for me in 1977 when he was about twenty-three, just married and very eager. I hired him because I knew his late father, Lee Floyd, who had lived in El Paso and had been the coach at Southern Mississippi. I've forgotten but Tim tells this one story all the time. He says on his first day he was a know-it-all twenty-three-year-old. I said I would show him around the new Special Events Center, our twelve-thousand-seat home gym. The first stop was the locker room and I guess he immediately suggested that we might consider putting some beanbag chairs and a television in the locker room so the players could hang out and relax. This has actually become all the rage today in college basketball, players' lounges, they call them. Practically every school has giant TVs and couches and all sorts of crap to entertain the players. Tim had seen the beanbag chairs somewhere and thought it might help recruiting.

He claims I looked at him and said, "Now why the hell would I want a player sitting on a beanbag chair watching television when he could be out on the floor practicing free throws?" Then he claims I told him to show himself around the rest of the building and I walked out. He didn't speak again for three months, which he claims made him a listener instead of a talker, a valuable skill for a young person in any profession. Well, I don't have much recall of that but I certainly can't argue with it; I mean, since when did players need lounges?

I do know Tim tried to modernize our recruiting. He was very organized, he worked very hard, he wrote lots of letters and, and this is the key thing, he was great with the mommas. No one can charm a mother like Tim Floyd. He was so good at it he'd have the mommas calling him. He'd tell them, "I am going to be getting your boy up at five-thirty in the morning and get him breakfast and then to class. I am going to make sure he graduates." And he did. Not just for a while either; he did it for nine years here. During that stretch there were only two guys who didn't graduate.

He would be at some house recruiting a new player and he'd have the mother of one of our current kids get in touch with the recruit's mother. I think Alice Davis, Antonio Davis's mother, was his best recruiter. Once the mamas are talking among themselves and they are saying, "Tim Floyd will make your boy go to school," well, you are in good shape. The NCAA didn't allow NBA players to call recruits, hell, North Carolina would have gotten everyone just by having Michael Jordan call. But they never said anything about the mamas. During the season all I did was concentrate on the team. By spring, Tim would hand me some plane tickets where I would visit the players and close the deal. He'd have the work all done. He'd say, "Just don't screw it up." Some families didn't even care if they met me, they'd say, "We'll send the papers in. You don't have to come." The ones I did visit, after I'd got there, I didn't know what the hell I was doin' there. It was already done. There wasn't much to say. This is why Tim will be so successful as the new coach at Southern California.

Even Tim could only offset our main problems so much. The first is publicity. Kids want to play on television and as good as the Western Athletic Conference was, we didn't have a lot of big media markets so we didn't get on TV that much. Plus, El Paso isn't a place the national media rolls through very often, so we were easy to overlook. Compounding this problem was our school's name. Winning the national title in 1966 made Texas Western a household name. People loved the name Texas Western, it just sounded good. But in the summer of 1966 Texas Western officially joined the University of Texas system and adopted the name the University of Texas, El Paso or UTEP, as it is commonly known. It was a good move for the school overall, but it didn't help me at all. I was calling around trying to convince kids that it was the same school that won the title a few months earlier. That really hurt.

El Paso itself is a tough place to recruit to. Recruiting is like real estate, the three most important things are location, location, and location. The single most important thing a program can have going for it is proximity to talent. You look at some of the historically great schools, the ones on the top ten all-time win list. But you'll also see places such as St. John's and Temple. Those aren't big schools with great facilities but there are players in the surrounding neighborhoods. And even the schools you don't think are close to talent actually are. Kentucky isn't a big state but there is Louisville, Cincinnati, Indiana, Ohio, Tennessee. It is a short flight to Detroit, Chicago, Washington, D.C., and Atlanta.

We are an eleven-hour drive from Dallas. Los Angeles and San Diego are actually closer than Houston. An advantage in recruiting is getting a player with his parents on your campus. When you are at Ohio State kids can drive over for a game, visit, get familiar with you. We could never do that. You had to fly here. And it is a long flight. The flight into El Paso is memorable because there appears to be endless deserts, mesas, and a whole lot of nothing. That isn't exactly appealing to a recruit from Los Angeles or Chicago. Tim Floyd came up with the idea of always flying them in and out at night, so they wouldn't realize just how remote it is.

I love El Paso but for these reasons I've envied some of my

coaching friends. When Bob Knight was at Indiana he always used to tell me, "I am going to get this one, this one, and this one." Because he could get him. Every year Indiana produced a few great players. If I had fifty towns around here with kids that good, I imagine we could have more consistently great players too. At UTEP we've had to take our chances on a lot of guys with the hope they would become great. I always told my assistant coaches, I would rather have a six-foot-six athlete than a six-ten guy with no talent. If a guy is an athlete, you have a better chance of making a player out of him.

It also helps when a coach's former players are coaches themselves at area high schools. Naturally, some of your players are going to get into coaching. If I had a great player when I was at Benjamin High School, don't you think Mr. Iba would have had the inside track? Recruiting that kid would have been simple. No one was better at this than Knight. Not only did his former players become coaches, but he'd tell me that every year he'd have around ten student managers who would go on to be high school coaches. After several years he had a guy in just about every town in Indiana. And I had that too. At one point I had a former player as head coach in each of the fifteen high schools in the city of El Paso. Unfortunately, not a single one of those schools had a player worth recruiting.

The key to recruiting for me was either to have a great assistant coach or, as I did in the earlier years, to have someone tip me off to an overlooked player. The best at that was Hilton White, my old friend from the New York playgrounds who sent three members of the 1966 national championship team to me. Hilton was the greatest, salt of the earth, and I remember right after we won the championship he called me about a little guard he had seen at DeWitt Clinton High School. I was tired after the season and didn't want to travel to New York, but Hilton told me if I didn't come watch this player he would never send me another one.

Well, that got me to New York. I watched DeWitt Clinton play Brooklyn's Erasmus Hall for the city championship. They played in a junior high school because the year before they had played in the city championship at Madison Square Garden and a big riot occurred. So the game was staged at a secret location. There were a bunch of coaches there, but they were all hanging on a six-foot-four guy named Walter Robinson who would go on to play at Loyola of Chicago. I immediately fell for Hilton's guy, a six-one, one-hundred-twenty-five-pounder named Nate "Tiny" Archibald. I couldn't believe I was getting that excited over a player that skinny but he was great. There was another player there too who impressed me, a guy named Mike Switzer. I couldn't believe neither of them were being recruited. That was the thing about these games in New York. You go watch and you didn't just find one player, you'd find three or four on a team. There was another guy on the team who came into the game who was six feet tall. I never saw a guy jump so high. He went to San Jacinto Junior College and then Guy Lewis at Houston got him and he jumped center. But he was just a sub on his high school team.

The only downside to players from New York is they usually can't shoot because they are used to playing on the playground, where the rims are bent. Guys from the suburbs learn to shoot because they have a basket on the garage. Kids from the ghetto don't get that. I brought Archibald in and told him that if he wanted to be a good player he would have to do it on his own, he'd have to find a place where he could shoot. He never said a word. But he started doing it. He was a hell of a workaholic. Mike Switzer was probably the more talented of the two. He could do it all. I don't remember anything he couldn't do. But I told him the same thing and he just looked at me. He didn't practice. He didn't like it enough. The story is one guy wanted to do it and one didn't. Tiny became a Hall of Fame player. Mike became a schoolteacher. Nothing wrong with that, Mike has had a very successful life and I'm proud of him, but that is how the sports world goes around.

As I said, after all of college basketball began recruiting black players, we struggled to get great basketball players here. They would go to bigger schools with more resources closer to their homes. We could recruit a kid for years, but if UCLA or Michigan came in at the last minute, he was gone. Instead we went for projects, guys who with a lot of coaching and hard work might pan out. When we signed Timmy Hardaway out of Chicago, he was a fat guard who couldn't shoot straight, but I liked his toughness. I think we beat Eastern Illinois for him. We were also good at finding good athletes and trying to make them into players.

I remember when Tim Floyd recruited Greg Foster from Oakland. Everyone was after Greg and he went to UCLA before transferring to UTEP. Tim kept talking about this unknown he had seen who nobody but the University of Portland was recruiting. He was a real skinny kid, about six foot seven, one hundred eighty pounds, who was seventh in his class academically. We were in town meeting with Foster and afterward went over to this unknown player's house. I am looking around the living room and the guy had nothing but swimming trophies and running trophies. Not a single basketball trophy. Later I chewed Floyd's ass out and accused him of being drunk. I said, "Tim, is it too much to recruit a *basketball* player?" The kid's mother was the smartest woman I ever talked to. She said, "Now, if he should come to your school, would you redshirt him?" To redshirt is to have the player voluntarily sit out the season. He gets to lift weights, practice, concentrate on school, everything but play in games. And he still has four years of playing eligibility. It is a great thing for most kids.

But I about fell off my chair when I heard it. A parent who wants her son redshirted? Usually you have to break it to the parents that their six-seven, one-hundred-eighty-pound son isn't going to be a starter. Redshirting allows a player to trade his worst season (his freshman year) for his best (an extra senior year, if you will). Parents almost never understand this. They think so highly of their son's ability they think he should start from day one. Just mentioning a redshirt season makes them think you are trying to put one over on them. So here is a mother smart enough to figure it out on her own. I loved her. Tim swore the kid could play, the mother was great, and I really liked the kid. Plus, I admit, I probably wanted recruiting to be over so I could go fishing. So I signed him. His name was Antonio Davis and he is still playing in the NBA today. About the only downside was his freshman season we had so many injuries I couldn't redshirt him. He had to play. But Antonio went on to be one of the greatest players I ever coached, mainly because he worked so hard, even after he made it to the NBA. Antonio is a self-made player and I like to think that the discipline he learned from swimming all those laps helped him concentrate on the repetition needed to become a better basketball player. Oh, and I never accused Tim Floyd of being drunk again.

FIFTEEN

EL PASO

In 2001, Haskins was scheduled to enter the hospital for some heart tests and, it seemed likely, another major surgery. He was in his seventies, already suffered from diabetes and had undergone open-heart surgery in the early 1990s. So he wasn't exactly what you'd call the strongest patient out there. The day before the hospital visit I flew down to El Paso to lift his spirits, along with two of his former assistants, Tim Floyd and Norm Ellenberger, who were both with the Chicago Bulls at the time.

What we found was Haskins in his normal state. Which is to say, even with the possibility of open-heart surgery the next

morning, he wasn't changing a damn thing and he certainly wasn't
sitting around having egg whites and grapefruit juice.

For lunch we went to this little Mexican restaurant and he got a
giant enchilada with a fried egg on top for good measure. By the
middle of the afternoon we were sitting around a bar, Haskins
knocking back whiskey. So we acted normal.

"Hey Coach," Floyd said, trying to tease him, "you ever take
any of that Viagra?"

Haskins looked incredulous.

"No, Tim, not with my health . . ."

■

I am often asked why I spent my entire career in El Paso.
Most coaches move around all the time. Very few would stick
around a place such as UTEP, which in reality does not have
enough resources or the recruiting base to compete with the
big schools. There are two reasons.

First, I love El Paso. We are in the high desert. The worst
weather we get is a sandstorm. We've never had a tornado
here. It doesn't rain much, which is the one thing I miss, but
you get accustomed to the desert. Yes, I'd see a rainstorm out
in the desert somewhere and I'd chase out there just to get
under it, but for the most part you get used to it. The hunting
is great—especially the white wing—and I love to hunt. But
really, it is the people that make up the town. The people have
been great to me. For the most part, they let me coach my

team. I've worked for some great people at UTEP. Even though I am retired every once in a while I have breakfast with our current president, Dr. Diana Natalicio, who has helped this university grow by leaps and bounds.

The second reason I stayed is because I never got into job hunts very much, which in some ways cost me. That is the part of coaching I never adapted to, it went from a job to a profession. If you want to feather your nest and get a better contract, then you have to act interested in job openings. I never really did that. I thought it was unfair to move kids around once you get them in school. I know guys do that all the time but I never wanted to do that. Mary was happy in El Paso and had more friends than she could count and I didn't want to break that up. We were comfortable in El Paso and that meant something to me. There was the time in the 1970s I took the head coaching job at the University of Detroit for one day, but once I got there I didn't feel comfortable with the people I would be working for, so I turned around, went back to west Texas, and never left.

For a while, after the championship, schools used to call every year with offers. But when you show no interest year after year, they stop calling. I remember in the early 1970s I got a call from Indiana and said no. They went on to hire Bob Knight. I don't know if I would have gotten the coaching job, but they called. New Mexico called on two or three occasions to see if I was interested. I damn near went to the Dallas Chaparrals, an ABA team, in the 1970s. But I never wanted to be a pro coach; the seasons were too long and there were too many games.

I was offered the job at Oklahoma State twice. I said no

both times because I wanted Moe Iba to get the job, but he didn't get hired either. Besides, I didn't want to succeed his father, Mr. Iba. I always thought it would be a great job and I know it has been fun for all the old Aggies to see one of our own, Eddie Sutton, return the program to the top. Eddie is a couple years younger than I am, but he played for Mr. Iba. When Eddie took over in 1990 the program was down, but they have gone to the NCAA tournament every year since he's been there and have even made it to a couple Final Fours.

Actually, one year I did do it. I was fed up with not getting a raise at UTEP so I took a trip to Lamar, of all places. The athletic director was a friend of mine who had been the associate here at UTEP before getting the job over at Lamar University, which is in Beaumont in east Texas. I had been down there to play and it wasn't bad. They had a nice twelve-thousand-seat place and they don't play football. I think I was tired of supporting football. We'd have a good year, football would go 1 and 10. I would ask if my assistants could get a raise. And they'd say, "No. We've got to get football up."

So I went to interview with Lamar. I didn't even meet their board or anything. The AD said, "We'll start you off with a $500,000 annuity." Then he offered a hell of a raise over what I was making. But I was about fifty-five, and I said, "Hell, this late in life, do I want to start new?" So I had to think about it. When I got back to El Paso I told a friend about it. The next day, and this is how that works, I was called over to the administrative building and they said, "You have a

$500,000 annuity." The only stipulation was if I quit, I would lose it. So I got that.

One thing that would have been easier if I had gone to a bigger school was scheduling. We always had trouble getting teams to come and play us. UTEP was one of those games coaches don't want to play. The coach knew we were always good enough to beat you, but the fans didn't. So if you beat us, you didn't get much credit. And if you lost, you got a lot of blame. That's the problem with fans, they think the only good teams and good players are on television. But teams get on television based on a league-wide contract. It used to happen to us also.

I remember one time in the early 1980s, Louisiana Tech was coming to town and I remember telling all the news media they've got a guy who is going to be in the NBA. And they all sort of laughed and thought I was exaggerating things, blah, blah, blah. Well, the guy I was talking about was Karl Malone, but he didn't have a very good game against us. We guarded him very well and he didn't do much. So then the fans and the media really didn't believe me, saying, "Yeah Coach, this Karl Malone is really going to be an NBA player."

The next week we were playing McNeese State. See, those schools from Louisiana always have some great talent but you can't sell it to people. McNeese State, what the heck is that? Who knew we even had a state named McNeese? Well, they had a guy by the name of Joe Dumars. So I told the media again, yeah, another guy who is going to be in the NBA. And everyone laughed, "Yeah, sure, Coach." Now I don't know if I ever had a guy make as many shots against us as Joe Dumars. He was making them from so far out they weren't threes, they were fours. He made some crazy shots. We beat them but it wasn't for a lack of effort by Dumars. I don't recall anyone laughing at me in the postgame press conference after that one.

That brings me to John Thompson, who coached Georgetown. What was happening in the early 1980s was we were getting shut out of the NCAA tournament. The NCAA loves the schools in the east, they'll take any ole team from the Big East. But a team from the west has got to do something special to get into the NCAA tournament. We kept going like 20 and 8, finishing second in the WAC and then getting snubbed. I'll never forget in 1981 we had a good team, built around a terrific center named Terry White. We won on regional TV in the last game in Wyoming's old War Memorial Stadium, a tough, tough place to play. We had a damn good team. If we had gotten into the NCAA tournament we could have won a couple games. But they didn't invite us. I raised hell for a couple weeks after that and then the NCAA said, "Well, it's your schedule." Well, it is always something. The NCAA has got a reason for everything. So I think that year almost everybody in the Big East went. So I told the media, "OK, schedule me the Big East."

Norm Ellenberger was the coach at the University of New Mexico then and we tried to get it going together. We offered teams to come out and play both of us, sort of make it geographically easy for them. We tried every school in the

Big East, but they all wanted us to play at their place and never to come out here. Finally, there was only one guy who agreed to play and that was John Thompson of Georgetown. They would come to El Paso once and we would go there twice. And we would use Big East officials in all three games, which would presumably give them some advantage. And of course I raised hell about that for a while, but what was I going to do?

Georgetown won the NCAA title in 1984 and reached the Final Four in 1985. The next season they came to El Paso. The Hoyas were ranked number five in the country and the Miner fans were so excited about the game that people slept out for tickets. We beat them by fourteen points. The next year we go to Georgetown and we were down two and had a shot at the buzzer but we missed two three-pointers within thirty seconds. So it was 1 to 1. We played them a last time in Washington, D.C., in 1990, when they had Alonzo Mourning and Dikembe Motumbo and were ranked number five again. We beat them by eleven. Those games meant a lot to our program and I always respected John Thompson for playing us when no one else would.

Well, I wouldn't say no one. Bob Knight brought Indiana to El Paso. Once, as a joke, we came out on the court together wearing each other's clothes. I had his red sweater on and he was wearing one of my gray sport coats. We had some good teams come out for our Sun Carnival Tournament also— Maryland, Villanova, Purdue, and some others played us. But overall, it was very tough to get a fair game with national teams. And since no one respected how good the WAC was, you couldn't leave your fate up to the NCAA selection committee. Even when you got in, they'd give you the hardest matchups imaginable.

In 1987, we went 24 and 6, were ranked nationally in the top twenty, and won the WAC regular season title. As a reward we played an NCAA tournament game against Arizona at Arizona. You got it, on their home court. We won in overtime, but how fair was that? It was the last time a team ever played on their home court in the tournament. The next night we had to play Iowa, who was ranked number six in the country and they had about twelve good players, including B. J. Armstrong and Brad Lohaus. They used to press defensively a lot then and we started out breaking their press and going down and shooting quick. You can't shoot quick against people who are pressing you unless you are better than they are. We weren't. But we kept getting out there three-on-two or four-on-three and the guys couldn't resist. We led 42 to 38 at the half, but in the locker room I was going crazy. I put the score on the board and I said, "We are ahead forty-two to thirty-eight and you don't understand we are getting our asses kicked." We were playing their game and eventually I knew they would beat us if we kept doing it.

It reminded me of the 1965 NCAA tournament. I was watching the games on television. UCLA, although a small team, had a hell of a bunch of shooters. They had that 2-2-1 full-court zone press John Wooden liked so much working for them. They were playing Michigan, which had a great All-American in Cazzie Russell. Michigan would break the press and about two passes, bang, they'd shoot quick. And they were making everything. They had UCLA down fifteen and I was sitting there watching it and I thought, as they kept doing it, they were fine. But you can't keep doing it and it wasn't long before Michigan was down fifteen. That's what I am talking about. You think John Wooden came out of the press when they were down fifteen? Hell no. He knew what was going to happen. It was fool's gold to hit those early shots. I sat there and watched and learned a few things. And that night against Iowa it came back to me. Once we started missing, everyone got scared and with about five minutes left in the game I couldn't get anyone to shoot. We got beat in a two-pointer and I'll tell you, we were good enough to make a hell of a run at the Final Four that year.

Sometimes I am not sure John Wooden gets all the credit he deserves as a coach. I know that sounds crazy because he is called the Wizard and all of that. A lot of people point out he had the best talent, he should have won. But I thought his philosophy was so good. They didn't particularly go out and get right in your jock because their man-to-man was almost like a zone, but you shot only once and he'd pick you up in that 2-2-1 press. He was never trying to get the ball with the press, but you might play too fast and give it to him. He just wanted you to come down the floor and shoot it a little too quick. And yes, he had Lew Alcindor and Bill Walton, but he won his first one with a six-foot-six center. UCLA always played with a lot of poise. They never got rattled. His saying was "Be quick, but don't hurry." I liked that. They played like that too. They played quick, but they weren't in a hurry to do it.

You see these teams who have all this talent, year after year they churn out NBA players, sign McDonald's All-Americans, have great depth, great athletes, and they never win the NCAA tournament. You have teams pound everyone during the regular season, get seeded number one year after year, and never win it. What is going on with those coaches? That's why Wooden deserves the credit. He won it ten times. When he was supposed to win it, he won it. You can't say that about a lot of other coaches.

I think the pressure gets to a lot of teams, a lot of coaches. Let me tell players and young coaches what I think is the most important thing about basketball. Don't ever play not to lose. You see it from teams all the time. They are just trying to run out the clock, not lose rather than trying to win. Nothing will cause you to lose quicker than playing scared, being afraid to make a mistake. Just play. If something bad happens, it happens. When you get to playing not to lose you are in trouble. Never play scared and always play hard and together; you are going to have a chance to win.

Although most of the attention from my career centers on the 1960s, we had some great teams and great players after that also. At one point during the 1980s we made six consecutive NCAA tournaments behinds guys such as Kent Lockhart, Jeep Jackson, Luster Goodwin, Chris Sandle, Juden Smith, Dave Feitl, Hardaway, and others. We really had the program going about as well as you can have it going in El

Paso. The most exciting thing to me was the reaction of the fans. We played in Memorial Gym during the championship year but eventually we moved to the larger Coliseum downtown (it seated twenty-five hundred more people) and then UTEP built the Special Events Center, which seated twelve thousand. The more people who could attend the games, the better it connected us with the city.

This meant a lot to me. Most of those people who came to watch us hadn't attended UTEP but they felt a part of the school. And I can't imagine how many of those kids running around felt that connection and wound up becoming students there. Our school is special—we have a large number of graduates who are the first in their family to attend college. A good portion are first-generation Americans to boot.

One of our best seasons came in the latter half of my career, in 1992. The year before we were a really good, but very young, team that had faded down the stretch. But I had high expectations because we returned a bunch of seniors, such as Marlon Maxey, David Van Dyke, and Prince Stewart, along with a junior named Eddie Rivera. That group was good enough to beat Georgetown at Georgetown when they were ranked fifth in the country. We put together a heck of a year, winning the WAC and entering the NCAA tournament at 25 and 6. We were really strong down the stretch, although we did lose at Air Force, which was mainly because their coach, Reggie Minton, was one of the very best I ever competed against. He's deputy executive director of the National Association of Basketball Coaches now, but Reggie got as much from his players as anyone I've been around, he just never had the chance to coach great players.

We were a nine-seed in the NCAA tournament, playing in Dayton, Ohio, and won a real ugly game against the University of Evansville in the first round. Both teams guarded the heck out of each other and maybe that made our second-round opponent, the University of Kansas, a bit overconfident. The Jayhawks were the number one seed, ranked number two in the country, and man, were they loaded. They had Adonis Jordan, Rex Walters, Alonzo Jamison, and a bunch of others. They were so gifted athletically that their defense took us completely out of our offense and they jumped out to an early lead. I had to switch to a gimmick offense, a kind of four corners that we hadn't practiced five minutes the entire season. It worked perfectly. Once we got it going they couldn't figure out how to stop us. We shot over fifty-eight percent in the second half, won 66 to 60, and moved on to the Sweet Sixteen.

Cincinnati was up next and they had two things going for them, guard Nick Van Exel, who we couldn't stop early, and coach Bob Huggins, who I am telling you can really, really coach basketball. We were down 16 to 4 and Van Exel was scoring at will on us. It was like the Kansas game; sometimes you are forced to do something different, make a quick change. Hell, if you're gonna get hung, you might as well try something. We switched to a triangle-and-two defense on Van Exel, which is to put two defenders on him and let our other three defenders guard the rest of the team. Prince

Stewart face-guarded Van Exel and we held him damn near scoreless the rest of the way. The problem with the triangle-and-two is you can't rebound out of the thing, which is why you hate playing it unless you are playing someone like Nick Van Exel and you have to. Cincinnati had a big kid named Jones who just killed us off the glass, he had twenty-four points. Late in the game Marlon Maxey got a tough offensive foul called on him and we wound up losing 69 to 67. UC went on to the Final Four and they were a deserving Final Four team. They were really good.

I don't want to spend a lot of time talkin' about the NCAA because it usually puts me in a bad mood when I do. All I can say is it is the most corrupt organization I have ever dealt with. They are so bought and sold by the big-money schools it isn't even funny. And it is generally run by a lot of people who don't know anything about sports and couldn't care less about the actual students. With the NCAA, it is just money, money, money.

What is interesting is that most people who spend their lives involved with the NCAA wind up hating the NCAA. They are the worst part of college sports. So much good comes out of college athletics. All the kids like me who got educations because of it. All the memories, the fun, the excitement for the fans. But the NCAA ruins as much of it as they can with their incessant money grab. It's painful to watch.

I was a college basketball player and coach combined for over four decades, almost my entire life was devoted to college athletics and all I wish is Congress would go investigate their asses. Then we'd see some stuff.

My 1992 team was the last one that really could have gotten back to the Final Four. We had some good, hardworking teams up until my retirement in 1999, but we never threatened the national tournament again. But that was OK. Winning for me was not everything. I know a lot of people who saw me on the sideline wouldn't think this, but it is true. And no, I didn't like losing, but a good effort was often just as important.

I had a two-year stretch in the late 1970s when we just weren't that good. But I had a great collection of kids, really smart students. There was Jimbo Bowden, who became a dentist here in El Paso, Tim Crenshaw, who is the president of a bank in town, and Steve Yellen, who is a vice president with Morgan Stanley Investments and the Miners' current radio color commentator. We won just eleven games a year during the 1977 and 1978 seasons, but after games I could sleep because my players had given every damn thing they had. Those were two of my four losing seasons, but I knew we were doing as well as we could. What bothers me most is underachieving.

We just didn't have a go-to guy. Then in 1979 we added a kid from town, Terry White, and we won twenty a year for the next few years after that. In 1979, even when we lost it was a down-to-the-wire game every night. I think I enjoyed that year more than even 1966. We'd play a Saturday night game somewhere, fly home on Sunday morning, and go right to the gym and you'd never hear a whimper. They were ready. And I was so proud of them the last two years, when they won twenty games. I knew I was very fortunate that I had good kids, good students. I also knew we could win only so much with nice kids. So it was then that I told Tim Floyd to go out and get me a couple pains in the ass to go with them.

SIXTEEN

RETIREMENT

Haskins has three grandchildren, the youngest of whom, Dominick, is now ten. At an early age Dominick took up the game of basketball and almost immediately took some coaching at his grandfather's knee. There Dominick was repeatedly told by arguably the greatest defensive coach of all time that the measure of a player was not how many points he scored, but how well he guarded his man.

A few years back Haskins and I were sitting around his kitchen table when Dominick and his father, Brent Haskins, came back from one of his very first games. Dominick was just six years old at the time and wasn't too happy.

"*Dominick got thrown out of the game for punching a kid,*" said Brent.

"*Why?*" *I asked.*

"*Well, Dominick was really intent on playing defense just like Grandpa showed him. He was guarding his man really closely on the defensive end of the court. But then, even when Dominick's team got the ball he kept guarding his man anyway. So Dominick was on offense, but still playing defense. The other kid got frustrated and punched Dominick. Then Dominick punched him back and the referee threw him out of the game.*"

Brent and I did all we could to stifle a laugh.

"*So he was covering a guy even when his own team had the ball?*" *I said to make sure I got it all right.*

Haskins had yet to say a word. As the concept of what happened sunk in, he quietly nodded his head, got the look of the proudest grandfather on earth, and wistfully declared, "Now that's what I call defense."

I used to play a lot of golf, although I can't anymore. Here I am retired, with all the time in the world to play golf, but with diabetes I can't get out and play. I still go down to Horizon or the El Paso Country Club and watch people play golf though, especially my son Steve, who is a professional golfer. I love golf and if there was one thing I did an awful lot of in El Paso it was play the game.

I remember one day in the early 1970s I was out at Horizon and we are fixin' to play golf. A farmer friend of mine, Martin Lettunich, was to play this other guy, Gene Fisher, who is also a great friend of mine. It was going to be a money game and it was going to be a good one. Well, Martin came walking up with a Mexican guy, about twenty-five years old, wearing dingy clothes. "Fellas," said Martin, "my tractor driver here says he can play a little, who wants to play him?" We all laughed at that. We knew better than that. We knew this guy must be pretty good. So we got the deal worked out, who was getting shots and so on. The problem Fish and I had is we didn't know just how good the Mexican guy was. Or maybe more accurately, we didn't know *who* he was. All I knew is we were getting whipped and on the eighteenth I said to Martin, "Your tractor driver is shooting sixty-four." The tractor driver pretended the whole time he couldn't speak English, but he could.

His name was Lee Trevino. Martin had big farms down in the valley so he could speak fluent Spanish. He found Trevino, who was an incredible talent but back then it wasn't easy getting on the PGA Tour as a Mexican. Still, I used to think, Who the hell is this guy? Well, one day Ray Floyd came through town. He had been on the tour, but had been suspended or something for throwing his clubs when he got mad. But he could play. They set up a money game between them. There were twenty or thirty of us watching, making all sorts of side bets, it was a big game. Those kinds of games go on all around the country. Well, Lee beat Ray Floyd's ass. We never doubted how good he was after that. Trevino never doubted himself in the first place, of course. He would always tell us how good he was. He'd say, "Watch this, no one can do this better than me." I think a golfer has to have that, has to have that confidence.

I remember one day Moe Iba and I went out to Horizon, where Lee got a job teaching, and he was standing in a sand pile practicing wedge shots. There weren't any sand traps out on the course so this is what he needed to do to make it. But we never thought the tour would let a Mexican play. I remember saying to Moe, "Damn it, that ole boy thinks he is going to play on the tour one day. I feel sorry for him."

Lee would make money any way he could. He was a natural hustler, but after a while no one in El Paso would play him. Then one day I remember him coming into the clubhouse and saying, "Coach, don't get involved in this, but we are going to do some arm wrestling." Like I said, anything to make a buck. So he is out there arm wrestling anyone who dared. For one buck you got an arm-wrestling contest with Lee Trevino. He was beating everyone, making everyone mad, and then finally one ole boy thought he had outsmarted him and said, "OK, Lee, I'll do it, but let's go left-handed." And Lee started hemming and hawing and said, "Only for ten dollars." He acted like he was hoping raising the bet would scare the other guy off. But it didn't, the guy gets all excited and lays ten dollars down. And, of course, Lee Trevino was left-handed. It was a hustle. He jerked the guy like nothing. Lee Trevino hustled in arm wrestling. He'd hustle anything.

I was a three or four handicap at my peak, which is pretty

good, but not as good as some of the big gamblers. Not that it really matters. The entire thing with bettin' on golf is what gets negotiated before you play. In most cases the outcome is decided before you leave the first tee box. Anyone can beat anyone if you are a good negotiator. And I have seen some of the best.

A lot of coaches play golf and a lot of them gamble. One guy who doesn't is Bob Knight. I once beat Knight out of fifty cents three ways and he calls me El Paso Ed to this day. Knight can't shoot pool either. He can coach. Actually, he has become a good fisherman, although many years ago he was about the worst fisherman I ever saw. Knight, Norm Ellenberger, and I went fishing and the only thing Knight caught all day was my hat. But you don't tell Knight he can't do something because he'll get good at it. And a few years later I was watching this fishing show that Knight was on. I figured it would be interesting because he can't fish. But he was good with that fly line. Real good. He had made himself a fisherman.

I spend a lot of time now following my son Steve, who is a great golfer and has been a professional for over twenty years. He has worked extremely hard at it and I am really proud of him. I am really proud of my entire family. It all comes from my wife, Mary. She is the best mother there's ever been and my two boys, Steve and Brent, are the best fathers I've ever met. I don't know where they learned that but it wasn't from me. I wasn't anywhere close to the devoted fathers they are. My oldest son, Mark, passed away when he was forty-two and David doesn't have any children, but I am very proud of all of them. I am just really lucky and I don't tell them that enough. But they are all just great boys. Mary did a great job raising the family. I didn't give enough time to them, I admit that. She did it all. She is the reason they are who they are. She taught them manners and it carried on in their lives. She is just incredible. I have three of the greatest grandchildren, John Paul, Cameron, and Dominick, who have ever been. All three of them are good students and interested in athletics. They are great kids.

One of the benefits of retirement is having some time to spend with my family. A coach's life is very demanding. There is always another game, another practice, another re-cruit to go and see. And when you bring these kids to town for college, you promise their parents that you'll be their par-ent in El Paso. That isn't an empty promise. You have to spend time making sure their lives are in order, dealing with whatever problems come up. You miss out on a lot of stuff with your own family. I missed a lot. I try to make up for some of that now.

As for my extended family—my former players—there isn't a day that goes by I don't get a couple calls from them. They call to check in, update you on their lives, and tell you what is going on. It is great to see how much success they have had. The 1966 team and I are particularly close, which is understandable. Be-fore Bobby Joe Hill died of a heart attack in 2002, he lived in El Paso, so I would see him a great deal. But I still talk often with Nevil Shed, David Lattin, Moe Iba, and many others. We have reunions and celebrations. The bond is still very strong. I think anyone could call anyone else on the team and even now, forty years later, it is like a day hasn't passed. We didn't know what we were doing then, I don't think any one of us could have predicted the impact, but we know now.

These days I don't do a whole lot. I like drivin' around, visitin' with some friends. It's a good life. I can still hunt, but only if I don't have to walk too far. My favorite now is shooting white wing, which we get millions of down here in the Southwest. White wing is a beautiful bird. It doesn't have much meat, but what there is is delicious, about the best-tasting pieces you've ever had. And I can hunt them because they all get out in a field you can drive up near. A friend of mine, Reece Lutich, has some land and there are lots of them out there. Otherwise if you find an old cornfield, they'll be there. These days I'd about as soon watch as shoot, but I still like to shoot some.

My friend Lo and I will drive up and get after them. I don't think I am ever happier than when I am hunting white wing. Some days there are so many of them, you just shoot until your shoulder hurts.

I attend just about all of UTEP's home games too. We have a terrific young coach, Doc Sadler, and the program is really going strong, reaching the NCAA tournament each of the last two years. I've gotten a real kick out of these teams because Doc is such a strong defensive coach. I have a lot of respect for the way he teaches the game. Plus there is a lot less stress watching a game than coaching it. It tends to make the evening more enjoyable.

Attending the games is a pretty good deal for me. They give me a parking spot just outside a back entrance and then they set me up with a chair on one baseline. I can kind of sneak right in. The only thing I don't like is when I arrive the PA announcer says, "Don Haskins is in the building." I'd rather not get any attention, especially if it diverts from the current players and the game. It's kind of like when they named the building after me, the Don Haskins Center. I guess that is a great honor and I appreciate it, but I would have preferred they just stuck with its original name, the Special Events Center. That made more sense to me. It wasn't just me who made that building or all those victories possible. It was a lot of players, assistant coaches, and so on.

For several decades now people in Hollywood have been comin' around talkin' about makin' a movie about the 1966 team. Nothing ever came of it until Jerry Bruckheimer and Disney got involved. It is really unusual to have people make a movie about your life, talkin' with an actor tryin' to be you. But I couldn't believe how great all of these people were to me and Mary. Jerry Bruckheimer is a big producer in Hollywood, but the way he dresses. . . . If he went into some of the local pubs in El Paso, they might not serve him. I mean that as a compliment. He is just a jeans and T-shirt guy. They filmed the movie in New Orleans, Baton Rouge, and El Paso. I went over to Baton Rouge to watch for a day and Jerry asked me to dinner. I was all worried I didn't have any clothes to wear. But hell, I turned out to be the best-dressed guy there.

The actor who is playing me in the movie is a guy named

Josh Lucas. Josh is so down-to-earth you can't believe it. I really enjoyed getting to know him. He came down to El Paso to meet me and we drove around a little and I got him drinkin' some tequila. I guess he was studying me, but it seemed like he was just having a good time. I got to know some of the other actors who were playing the players and they were great too. Tim Floyd actually coached the actors, tried to make them look more like basketball players. Then there was the director, Jim Gartner, who is as nice of a man as you'd ever want to meet.

When they were filming in El Paso, they told me they wanted me to appear in a cameo. I said no way I was doing that. I really had no interest in being in the movie, even just a little part like they had in mind. But then Jim Gartner called about three days before the scene was going to get filmed and said, "Don, we were expecting you to do it, almost everyone wants to." Well, I didn't want to do it, but here was the thing— I respected how hard they all worked on that movie. I didn't know directors, actors, writers, and all the crew worked that hard. These guys really worked to make it a good movie. When you are sittin' home watching a movie on TV, know that a lot of hard work went into it. So because Jim asked, I agreed to do it.

The scene had Josh Lucas at a pay phone at a gas station. We filmed it out in Fabens, Texas, not far from El Paso. Josh Lucas is me and I'm me, but I'm playing a gas station attendant named Don. When he is on the phone, my line was: "Do you want me to fill your tank?" I got it right the first time and thought, That's that, I'm done. I was ready to get out of my gas station attendant uniform and get a drink. But they film these damn scenes about fifty times, I guess they want to make sure everything is perfect. It felt like practicin' for Mr. Iba all over again. So I kept havin' to do my line over and over. After about the seventh take I turned to Jim Gartner and said, "That's it, you've got my best work." He just laughed and said, "OK, OK." He let me off.

So what do you know, after all these years, I guess I'm an actor now.

ACKNOWLEDGMENTS

There is no way to thank all the people who helped with this book, but we'd like to mention a few.

First, from Coach Haskins:

My parents, Paul and Opal Haskins; my brother, Jerry; and my cousin, Shirley Haskins, who is still up in Enid, provided me the foundation for life.

Mr. Henry Iba and Dale Holt, who not only taught me basketball but how to be a man.

Moe Iba was my assistant coach on the 1966 NCAA

Championship team and is one of the finest men and coaches I have ever known. He was as color blind about players as I was and deserves every bit the credit I have received. He was a great young coach then was absolutely the best scout I still have ever seen. A few years later, Gene Iba, Mr. Iba's nephew, became my assistant—another Great Iba mind.

Tim Floyd came to me as a twenty-two-year-old graduate assistant. He was a tireless worker and a great recruiter. During his time in El Paso he totally turned UTEP basketball around. In his nine years, we had only two players who didn't graduate. Tim went on to be a great coach in college and the NBA and is now at Southern Cal. He is one of my dearest friends.

Thanks to Bob Knight, who in the next couple of years, health permitting, will be the first NCAA coach to reach 900 wins. This will prove that he is the greatest basketball coach of all time. Bob, thanks for writing the foreword and being a good friend through the years.

George McCarty, Ben Collins, and Dr. Joe Ray believed in me when I was just a small-town high school coach and helped start everything. J. R. Yell hired me at Dumas High School when nobody would give me a shot at a bigger school. Without that, I am not sure coming to Texas Western would have been possible.

Kathy Beilharz, Marge Williamson, and Diana Giddens were my secretaries through the years who managed to keep me as organized as possible.

Dr. Diana Natalicio is the current president of UTEP

and has done wonders for the school and the city and has been incredibly nice to me.

Throughout the years I have been blessed with great friendships with some of the team doctors, who have unselfishly given their time and talents and traveled with our team. Dr. Billy Dickey, Dr. Hampton Briggs, and Dr. Bob Schneider were there, among many others.

If I had ever paid Bill Eschenbrenner of the El Paso Country Club and Danny Swain of the Coronado Country Club for all of the golf lessons they provided, it would have been too much to count. Both country clubs have given my entire family life memberships. I also want to thank a third country club, Vista Hills, where I spent many, many days and where Terry Jennings is the pro.

Fred Schneider, owner of the Pontiac dealership, was the first car dealer to provide a courtesy car to me. He also sponsored my son, Steve, in professional golf. I also want to thank Wally and Clay Lowenfield of Casa Ford for providing a courtesy car for many years for my wife, Mary.

For about thirty-eight years I have been very fortunate to drive a GMC pickup provided by Travis Crawford. Even after my retirement in 1999 he still provides me with a GMC pickup. I don't know of any other coach who, after retirement, is still provided with a vehicle.

My health had been good until recent years. I have had two open-heart surgeries by Dr. Joe Kidd, one of the world's best. I will forever be grateful for the wonderful care given to me by Dr. George Didonna, Dr. David Gough, Dr. Gregory

Szeyko, Dr. Charles Lyon, Dr. Al Hernandez, Dr. Bob May, and Dr. Dwayne Aboud.

Thanks to all of these men for their kindness.

All of my former players and assistant coaches, who are too numerous to name but have a special place with me. Also thanks to all the guys I played with at Enid High School and Oklahoma A&M.

I have been lucky to have some incredible friends, including the Stretch Elliott Family; my athletic directors, Jim Bowden, John Thompson, Ed Schwartz, and UTEP's current athletic director, Bob Stull. My friends have been with me through thick and thin.

I could go on, but maybe just printing the El Paso phone book would be briefer.

From Dan Wetzel:

A number of players, coaches, administrators, and friends of Coach Haskins were invaluable in selflessly helping me with this story and keeping Haskins's memory sharp (or honest). They include Nevil Shed; Willie Worsley; Harry Flournoy; Bobby Joe Hill; Herman Carr; Steve Tredennik; Nolan Richardson; Andy Stoglin; Moe and Gene Iba; Tim Floyd; Eddie Sutton; Earl Estep; Steve Yellen; Jeff Darby; Mary, Brent, and Steve Haskins; Bill Berryhill; Gene Fisher; Glenn Keller; Robert Brown; Wing Lo; Jeff Limberg; Humberto Fournier; and Eddie Mullens.

Our talented editor at Hyperion, Kiera Hepford, was both diligent with direction and a master at helping us keep the narrative as clean, yet as colorful, as possible. She was a better and far more patient editor than the two of us deserved.

At the William Morris Agency in New York, Manie Baron believed in this project originally and later Jonathan Pecarsky brought it together in what will hopefully be the first of many great projects to come. As an added bonus, he learned more about El Paso than he ever imagined possible.

My former editor at Yahoo! Sports, Sam Silverstein, gave the manuscript a detailed read when he certainly had more pressing things to do. The same applies to former Miner Steve Tredennik, who saved us on countless factual errors. Ron Wilson brought a great perspective to the final draft to make Pellston (Michigan) High School proud.

Thanks as always to friends and colleagues David Scott, Michael Morrissey, Adrian Wojnarowski, Ian O'Connor, Mike Vaccaro, Pete Thamel, Charles Robinson, Jeff Shelman, Don Yaeger, Dick Weiss, Andy Katz, Mike DeCourcy, Mike Rosenberg, Mike Sheridan, Brian Murphy, Paul and Matt Tryder, John Berry, and Pat Mungovan.

Larry Donald of *Basketball Times* originally sent me to El Paso to interview Don Haskins, and for that and so much more I will be forever indebted.

The work of Ray Sanchez and Frank Fitzpatrick, both of whom wrote terrific books on the 1966 team, as well as Alexander Wolff of *Sports Illustrated*, were leaned on for research and fact checking. Bill Knight of the *El Paso Times* is a great journalist and friend, as is Steve Kaplowitz of KROD Radio.

My parents, Mary Ellen and Paul Wetzel, are supportive of everything I attempt, and I can't begin to convey my appreciation for that.

Finally, there is no way this book (or just about anything I do) could have been accomplished without my wife, Jan, who deals with late nights, early mornings, last-minute flights, and a frantic schedule that makes no sense. In this case, all while bringing our wonderful daughter, Allie, into the world. She is also the finest line editor I have ever known and is my most brutally honest (a much appreciated trait) critic. She is just incredible.